THE POND LOVERS

The Pond Lovers

BY GENE LOGSDON

The University of Georgia Press   Athens and London

© 2003 by the University of Georgia Press
Athens, Georgia 30602
All rights reserved
Designed by Sandra Strother Hudson
Set in Bembo by Graphic Composition, Inc.
Printed and bound by Maple-Vail
The paper in this book meets the guidelines for permanence
and durability of the Committee on Production Guidelines
for Book Longevity of the Council on Library Resources.

Printed in the United States of America
07 06 05 04 03 C 5 4 3 2 1

Library of Congress Cataloging-in-Publication Data

Logsdon, Gene.
The pond lovers / by Gene Logsdon.
p. cm.
Includes bibliographical references (p.).
ISBN 0-8203-2469-8 (hardcover : alk. paper)
1. Farm ponds. 2. Ponds. I. Title
S494.5.W3 L64 2003
631—dc21
2002151286

British Library Cataloging-in-Publication Data available

For

JOHN BASKIN

my favorite mentor

CONTENTS

Acknowledgments | ix

Introduction | 1

The Pond at the Center of a Family's Universe | 4

A Pasture Pond | 16

A Modern Thoreau beside a Modern Walden Pond | 37

Andrew Wyeth's Pond | 50

The House of Seven Ponds | 61

An Amish Bishop's Swimmin' Hole | 70

Jandy's Pond | 77

A Wild Food Gatherer's Garden Pools | 86

Hillside Catchment Ponds | 93

Ponds as Sustaining Food Cupboards | 103

Ponds and Sustainable Technology | 125

Strings of Pearly Pools | 139

Shambaugh Pond | 154

Appendix | 163

ACKNOWLEDGMENTS

When I look back over the many years that I was unconsciously gathering the material and experiences that would eventually result in this book, I realize that I should thank a small army of people, many of whom have passed away. My grandfather Henry Rall comes to mind first because he provided me with one of my most vivid pond-related memories when he drained his farm pond to repair the dam. I watched with total fascination as large fish, washed out in the overflow, tried to swim down the sheep paths below the dam. My father, Gerald, I must surely mention. He built the pond on the home farm that is featured in the first chapter and, more than anyone else, instilled in me the love of ponds. Donald Hall, a friend of my younger years and under whom I worked in the Soil Conservation Service, taught me most of what I know about the technical aspect of designing farm ponds. Dale Shambaugh, although gone now like the aforementioned, needs a special thanks, for were it not for him the magical ending of this book might not have happened. Besides, he always encouraged my writing in the local newspaper, even when what I was writing irritated many readers.

I thank all the people who cooperated in allowing me to write about them and their ponds. They are, individually and together, most amazing characters. I pray that I have done them justice in the writing.

The first chapter of this book appeared in somewhat the same form in an earlier book, *Living at Nature's Pace,* from Chelsea Green Publishing, White River Junction, Vermont. Some of the information in chapter 10, "Ponds as Sustaining Food Cupboards," I learned while working for Rodale Press, Emmaus, Pennsylvania, and wrote about in *Organic Gardening* magazine and in one of my Rodale Press books, *Getting Food from Water,* published in 1978 and now out of print. Some of the material in chapter 11, "Ponds and Sustainable Technology," I learned about while working for JG Press, Emmaus, Pennsylvania, in the early 1990s and wrote about during that time in its magazines, *BioCycle* and *In Business.*

And finally, thank heavens for Barbara Ras, executive editor at the University of Georgia Press, for recognizing that a book merely of instruction about building and maintaining ponds, of which there are already too many, was only half the story. Pond lovers themselves were the other, and more important, half.

THE POND LOVERS

INTRODUCTION

Some mysterious attraction draws me to any body of water larger than a hot tub. Like the hero in the classic science fiction novel *Stranger in a Strange Land,* I "grok" water. My clearest childhood memory is of our family's annual trip to Lake Erie, sixty miles from our landlocked farm. I can still feel the rush of excitement as we approached the lake and the trees finally gave way to a seemingly limitless expanse of shimmering water. Most of my life I have fantasized about living on islands, or seashores, or on a shanty boat floating forever on a river of no return. I have a recurring dream that must come out of genetic memory, because I have never experienced in real life what happens in the dream. I am standing at the bow of a boat, like Washington crossing the Delaware, as it sails out of the mouth of a little creek into a vast river, the sight of which fills me with utter awe and happiness. I wonder how the Freudians would interpret that.

As a landlocked midwesterner, I made the most of what was available. I began a lifelong love affair with farm ponds. I helped build them and learned to maintain them. I swam in them, boated and skated on them, fished and hunted beside them. Most of all, I just watched nature unfold around them and learned that a pond could be a sort of reflection of the whole world, the sky mirrored on its surface, the water drawing to it like a biological magnet, a seemingly limitless fund of life. I became aware of just how awesomely productive of food, water, beauty, and ecological health the environment of a pond could be, with its surrounding grassy pasture and, perhaps, a bit of woodland. If repeated over the entire countryside, a half-acre pond for every hundred acres of farmland could result in food independence for any region as well as a sustainable environmental paradise for everyone living there.

Only then did I realize something perfectly obvious. Small pools of water in every garden could bring the same human and ecological benefits to urban areas as a farm pond and pasture landscape could to rural areas. These benefits could be attained by engaging in rather pleasant tasks and mostly recreational fun, not investing hard work or big sums of money. What people could gain by just staying home and making an enjoyable life there, rather than thundering down the highways hell-bent on seeing how much fuel they can burn, would alone be of significant value to society. Add to that the immeasurable social benefits of the tranquillity that a pool of water can cast upon the human soul, and one has reason enough to build ponds without considering their direct benefits.

Obviously other people feel the same as I do: the number of artificial ponds being built is dramatically increasing, as farm pond and garden pool supply businesses will be only too glad to tell you. From where I sit writing this, I can think of a dozen farm ponds within a mile radius and twice that many in the next mile radius. And more are being built. In towns and cities, garden pools are multiplying even faster. The attraction to water is in our genes, and people are realizing that they can maintain a garden pool almost as easily as a lawn and enjoy their own little vacation lake, or island, or seashore, or wilderness area right in their own backyard.

So I started to write this book to share the good news and to add my experiences to the developing knowledge of farm pond and garden pool management. What I've learned doesn't always agree with the manuals bent on separating you from your money in the name of enhancing or maintaining your pond for breathtaking beauty or for increasing its production of fish or other water-borne life to an unnatural level. Going that direction brings no argument from me, but my ideal is a pond that sustains itself without adding fertilizers, chemicals, or even aeration equipment, as the maintenance manuals so often call for. I've compromised by talking about both approaches but not to the extent of including much about commercial aquaculture. That is a risky business and does not necessarily lead to the tranquillity I seek from ponds. The farm pond or garden pool that I favor in this book is to commercial aquaculture precisely what a garden is to commercial farming.

Not long after I got into the book and started visiting other pond owners, I realized that pond lovers are often extraordinarily interesting people in character and point of view. I decided that the best way to pass on really good information about small bodies of water was to describe these people and their relationships to their ponds. The book turned from an instructional manual into something a whole lot more important: a work about the why-to as well as the how-to. If you are after only instructional material, you can just skip a couple of the chapters that discuss the cultural rather than aquacultural benefits of ponds.

Humanizing the instructional material also led to some rather startling discoveries about ponds and garden pools that I had not foreseen as integral to the book. Ponds are being used worldwide for everything from stopping starvation in Africa to imaginative new ways to turn polluted water into clean water while growing useful water plants and animals in them.

The result has been, I hope, a book that gives helpful instruction about building, maintaining, and enjoying small bodies of water while offering a literary appreciation of their social and environmental values. Something else emerged that I had not exactly foreseen: a message of environmental hope in a world that sorely needs it.

THE POND AT THE CENTER
OF A FAMILY'S UNIVERSE

The man standing stone-post still on the shoreline of the Pond was watching a swimming muskrat, its wake forming a V-shaped ripple of scarlet fading into indigo against the sunset. Without turning his head, which might scare the muskrat into diving underwater and scooting for its den, the man also noted, out of the corner of his eye, a great blue heron drifting down out of the sky toward him. He was used to seeing the heron on its nightly trip up the creek valley, headed back for the rookery where most of our county's herons, silent and solitary by day, gathered to roost. But this time the huge slate-gray bird, its wingspan more than five feet, was doing something that wary great blue herons do not normally do. It continued to drift down in the twilight, made a pass over the water, and then turned straight at the man as if to land on one of the posts that held the homemade pier he was standing on. Forgetting the muskrat but still not moving a muscle, the man watched aghast as the great bird hovered above him, like an avenging angel, and perched *right on the top of his head.*

Not many people would have the steely nerves to suffer, without moving, a great blue heron's talons gripping his head, but this man, my brother-in-law, is not known in these parts for reacting to anything in an ordinary manner. He had already realized that no one was going to believe him unless he caught the bird. He inched his right hand up the side of his body. Slowly, slowly, slowly. Gotcha! With one swift grab he snatched the heron's legs in his hand like a chicken thief taking a hen from the roost, and he bore his prize homeward so that all the neighborhood might see and believe. His family gathered round, ignorant of the danger involved. None of them knew that great blue herons can skewer an unsuspecting human's eyeball right out of its socket with one lightning stab of its beak. Fortunately, this bird's captor wore glasses, and when the heron jabbed at him, it only knocked the glasses from his head. When another onlooker reached for the glasses, the heron speared him in the hand, having endured, it seemed, enough human attention for one day. A quick decision was reached: in the case of herons, better two in the bush than one in the hand. The bird haughtily stalked away, looking like the dignified old lady who hoped no one had been watching when the wind momentarily blew her dress over her head. Then it pumped its wings up and down, slowly lifted itself into the air, and flew away.

Life at the Pond, as we have always called it, has been full of such adventures. One of my sisters, who lives where she can see the Pond from her windows, once watched a cormorant repeatedly waddle out on the diving board, raise its wings slightly in the way cormorants do, and dive in. My sister assumed that the bird was diving for fish, but she was not sure. "It looked exactly as if it were practicing for the Olympics," she says.

Another day, I arrived at the Pond for a hockey game to see about a dozen little nieces and nephews sprawled out, faces down on the ice. My first thought was that they had finally killed one another in a grand hockey massacre. Closer examination, however, revealed that they were peering down through the crystal-clear ice at a trio of snapping turtles with carapaces as big as meat platters, clearly visible scarcely two feet below, lolling on the pond bottom as if it were June. I joined the curious children. If we all lay there without movement, fish would congregate under our bodies, obeying an instinct to hide under logs, which they mistook us for. The ice had become a giant television screen, tuned to nature's own PBS station.

Three generations of our family have worked, played, fought (the only verb that properly describes our hockey games), picnicked, swum, camped out, made out, and celebrated holidays around the Pond. Most of all, it has been a haven where any of us could come when the need to be alone hit us, to sit and slip out of the consciousness of self and into the arms of a little watery wilderness that thrums and hums with enough activity to keep a naturalist occupied for a lifetime or two.

A pond surrounded by meadow and with a grove of trees growing nearby attracts and concentrates an amazing diversity of wildlife. In this humdrum Corn Belt county of north central Ohio, the Pond has hosted, by my count, more than forty different kinds of wild animals, not counting hockey players. In addition, we have identified at least 130 bird species around, on, or above the Pond. I have not begun to learn the names and numbers of different insects, the most fascinating pond wildlife of all. I watch for the coming of a little water bug, for example, by the name of *Hydrocampa propiralis,* which likes to eat the leaves of waterweeds. However, it can't swim or is too lazy to try, and so, like a good American, it uses technology instead. It builds itself a tiny boat out of bits of leaves and sails off into the wild blue yonder.

As I play Thoreau and watch the life of this little wilderness in action, there evolves in my inner vision a scene of seething, roiling, dynamic consumption. The Pond is an endless, entwined, labyrinthian dining table, at which sit the eaters being eaten. Barbaric as that vision seems, it is the accurate view of nature, a view without which ecology remains only a vague word, incomprehensible to both the environmentalist who wishes to protect nature and the entrepreneur who wishes to subdue and exploit nature. The Pond teaches that life is not so much a progression from birth to death as a circle of eating and being eaten, the chemicals of one body passing on to form another. A frog becomes a charming prince, not by a kiss but by the magic of the biological chain of life.

I sit on the bank and peer into a clump of cattails. As Yogi Berra gets credit for saying, "You can observe an awful lot just by watching." A muskrat chomps on the rhizomes at the bases of the cattails. The rhizomes are good for humans, too, if cooked like potatoes. The young pollen spikes, steamed, are offered as gourmet food in fancy restaurants, and "ears" of this "cattail corn" sell in specialty West Coast supermarkets. However, the muskrat must enjoy its delicacy with one eye over its shoulder, watching for mink, for whom muskrats are a delicacy. The mink, in turn, had better be alert for the great horned owl nesting in the woods next to the Pond. The owl is not at all deterred by the odorous oil that the mink can unleash, skunklike, when disturbed, and Mrs. Great Horned Owl's young would appreciate a change of diet from the red-winged blackbirds she has lately been snatching off the cattails, where the birds roost.

Sunfish hide among the cattails, where they hope the big bass will not find them. The sunfish look for snails to eat, and the snails in turn are feeding on algae. If the sunfish watch out only for bass, they may not notice the little eastern green heron standing like a statue at the shoreline, ready to grab and gobble them. And if they elude both bass and heron, the kingfisher, which sits on the dead branch of the shoreline hickory tree, may dive-bomb into the water and spear them. If the kingfisher isn't around, beware of cormorants practicing for the Olympics.

The algae, meanwhile, compete with the cattails for nutrients in the wastes dropped by muskrat and heron and redwing. A frog sits among the cattails too, hidden half by them and half by its own camouflage colors. The frog doesn't know that the cattails and the other pondweeds protect it from predators. The plants just make a convenient place to hide while it waits to snatch flying bugs attracted by the pondweeds' flowers. On the upper stalk of a cattail, a dragonfly perches, waiting patiently to make dinner of a mosquito buzzing by. In the pond, dragonfly larvae feed on mosquito larvae, while fish feed on both. Attached to the cattail stalks under the water, often in symbiotic nutritional relationship with them, are diatoms and blue-green algae being eaten not only by the snails but by various insects and worms. Other types of algae—filamentous algae drifting in the water—become food for bullfrog and toad tadpoles. The snapping turtles, themselves being parasitized by leeches sucking their blood, will eat some of the bullfrog tadpoles, and humans will eat some of them after they grow up to be frogs. And, by and by, if I am not too lazy to do the butchering, humans will eat a turtle too.

Even those plants and animals that die a "natural" death—the most unnatural death of all—do not escape the feast at nature's table. Bacteria "eat" the ammonia produced by decay and turn it into nitrites. Still other bacteria turn the nitrites into nitrates. The algae and plankton then eat the nitrates and turn them into proteins. Microscopic animals eat the microscopic plants, and the proteins, carbohydrates, and minerals in them begin the long climb up through the biological food chain. If that sounds complicated, understand that I am oversimplifying the process exceedingly.

The largest or must cunning eaters at the head of the table are kept from destroying the whole food chain because they are the most vulnerable to changes or shortages in the menu—as the dinosaurs proved. The exception to the circle of diners is the rational human, who is clever enough to find sustenance in almost any part of the food chain, but who also has the chilling freedom to rise above it, to act against nature. Thus humans, when they do not understand the full impact of their awesome powers, become nature's greatest danger.

As I watch, the Pond becomes a giant magnet attracting the wildlife around it. The barn swallow skims the surface of the water for bugs; the raccoon and opossum fish from the shoreline; the deer come down to the water for a drink; a black rat snake basks in the sun, having already raided a redwing's nest and satiated its hunger. A cedar waxwing flutters above the water for bugs. A wood duck floats on it, diving for food. A flycatcher darts out over it and back again to a tree. A buzzard soars high above it all, watching me, hoping that my stillness means I'm dying and that it can get me before the undertaker does.

My father built the Pond in 1950, with his little Allis Chalmers WD tractor and its hydraulic manure scoop substituting for a bulldozer. Whether he knew it or not—not having any technical engineering experience in such matters except his own common sense—he picked an almost perfect spot for a farm pond. About a quarter of an acre in size, the Pond drains water from a watershed of barely ten acres—an ideal ratio. Almost all of the land draining into it is woodland, so that no silt-laden water from cultivated farmland, saturated with fertilizers and toxic chemicals, can wash into it. Most amateurs want to build a pond that catches the runoff from many more acres than that, which means a large dam and water area, hard to take care of properly, plus an expensive catch-basin drain and spillway pipe and a large emergency grass spillway to keep water from overflowing and washing away the earthen dam. The Pond has no concrete catch-basin spillway at all, but only an emergency spillway off to the side of the dam. Despite expert opinion to the contrary, the little spillway has proved to be adequate, barring a catastrophic flood. The Pond, with its earthen dam, is called technically an embankment pond. Embankment ponds like ours are especially practical in gently rolling country where small ravines cut through low hills. Dams in this terrain are relatively small and so not prohibitively expensive.

Neighbors stopped by during the summer construction work on the Pond to speculate about when, or if, it would fill with water. Uncle Ade finally reached a verdict.

"Won't fill for two years," he wailed. He always talked as if he had to drown out the roar of a mufflerless tractor.

"And it'll dry up every August," Uncle Lawrence chimed in.

Dad, who did not get along very well with either Lawrence or Ade—or, come to think of it, anyone else—paid no attention to them as he scooped the dirt out of the ravine and pushed it onto a pile for the dam. The Pond was full by Thanksgiving.

The Soil Conservation Service agent also stopped by to cast dubious eyes on the project. He offered to survey and design the dam properly, which Dad took as a kind of effrontery.

"Don't need government help," he said.

"But if you let us design it, the government will pay a third or more of the cost," the technician explained.

"Yeah, and if I do it your way, it will cost me a third more to build," Dad snorted.

As a result of Dad's stubbornness, our dam leaked a little, not having a properly packed clay core in the center base of it. The dam should have been wider, too, at least ten feet across the top, but with some bulking up over the years where muskrats have tried to dig holes through the dam, it has neither washed away nor gone dry in fifty years.

Dad would not take the wildlife experts' advice on stocking the Pond, either. The standard stocking practice in those days was so many largemouth bass to so many bluegills. Dad maintained that any bluegills at all would lead to their overpopulation, no matter how many bass were present to eat them or how hard the Pond was fished. The wildlife experts sniffed in disagreement, but I remember one day a few years later when we caught ninety-eight bass weighing between half a pound and a pound. When I'm hungry for fish, which is often, I'll settle for that, even though bluegills taste a mite better. Other kinds of fish did eventually get into the Pond anyway, either from fishermen dumping out their minnow cans or as eggs on the feet of water birds or because other family members put them in.

We did take the government's advice and planted multiflora roses for "living fences" around the Pond. They turned out to be living hells of briers. I have not much listened to expert advice since then.

The Soil Conservation Service had more luck with citizens less contrary than my father, which would include nearly everyone except me. Even if its multiflora rose and autumn olive programs are turning many Ohio pastures and woodlots into living hells of briers, the service can boast justifiably that by 1990 it had designed and helped build an estimated nine thousand artificial ponds and small lakes in Ohio alone. The number in other states is comparable. No one seems to know how many artificial ponds there are today, because a large number of new ones have been built without SCS assistance. The federal pond-building program, probably the most beneficial government effort for the public good ever funded, has been all but dropped.

The reason the government funded farm ponds was their environmental benefits. In some cases they slow the runoff of water to rivers, alleviating the effects of sudden floods and decreasing the amount of soil erosion. The water that is held back helps recharge groundwater. Meanwhile, water in ponds continually evaporates back into the atmosphere to help recharge the hydrologic cycle. Ponds further benefit society by taking out of cultivation land that often should not be farmed anyway: ravines and hillsides and low spots that profit-squeezed farmers would otherwise be planting in erosive grain crops. Also, ponds near houses and barns can be used for fire protection. Many ponds are used as a source of house and drinking water when well water is too high in sulfur or polluted. On farms where creeks or springs are not present, ponds are often built for livestock water. Some ponds are also used for irrigation.

But although Dad was full of ideas for growing fish commercially in our pond and using the water, enriched with fish manure, to irrigate a super-duper market garden below the dam, the Pond has been used only for recreational purposes. It has been the symbolic, if not real, center of our family's activity for years, the center of our universe. Five of my siblings' homes are more or less clustered around the Pond. Next to the Pond lies what looks like a large lawn today, but for years its identity was given away by the bare spots where the bases and pitcher's mound were located. In summer as we grew up and then our children grew up, we played softball there. In fall we switched to football and then in winter to the hockey wars. A pier and diving board inevitably appeared at the Pond, and then a sandy bit of beach and a small apron of concrete on the shoreline so that the children could splash without stirring up mud. Steel posts set in the concrete apron held a net to keep children from wandering into deep water. In winter the posts stuck dangerously above the ice to provide yet another hazard to the hockey wars.

Muddy bottoms are characteristic of most farm ponds, which is why piers get built and eventually a raft gets anchored in the middle of the pond. One of my cousins, who happened to own a stone quarry in those days, decided he would dump a few loads of crushed stone into his pond to make a mudless bottom. Ton upon ton upon ton he dumped. The stone just seemed to disappear into the bowels of the pond, covered over not only with dirt but with the pond slime that invariably coats the bottoms of farm ponds fed by runoff water. The beach he made needed almost yearly additions of sand, too. He finally became convinced that, even with his own stone quarry, it was costlier to try to turn a farm pond into a swimming pool than to build an in-ground concrete swimming pool.

The site of his pond, known as Eagle Park for at least three-quarters of a century, was the center of my mother's family universe and the scene of the original hockey wars, before they moved two miles away to the Pond. We know that the Eagle Park pond existed at least as early as 1879, because it is marked on the old maps. It was built for winter ice to supply the local restaurants and saloons. One of my neighbors, now passed away, always maintained that farming was a lot more profitable before refrigerators.

The wars at Eagle Park involved the whole rural and village community and were dominated by my parents' generation, especially Uncle Lawrence, who flew up and down the ice on racer skates, the blades of which were at least fifteen inches long. To keep playing hockey after dark, we soaked straw bales in used oil and burned them, one behind each goal.

One afternoon, Uncle Lawrence, bored with hockey, drove his old wooden-spoked truck out on the ice and skidded around in giddy circles, whooping like a kid. He finally overdid it and slammed the truck into the bank sideways so hard that one of the wooden wheels snapped in two. Undaunted, he fetched from the nearby hickory grove a tree branch with a proper curve to it and wedged it in under the axle to serve as a sort of sled runner in place of the wheel. Still whooping, he drove the jalopy a mile to his farm.

Eagle Park in the 1920s and '30s really was a park, with a baseball diamond as well as the large pond for fishing and swimming and the grassy grove of hickories for picnicking. Across the road from it was a little red-brick schoolhouse, fallen down today, which I suppose was the reason that the park came into existence in the first place. Grandfather Rall did not care for such frivolous notions as providing the community with a park. He valued the pond because his sheep needed water. He drained the pond once to work on the dam, and even though I was only a little boy then, I can still remember big catfish wriggling down the sheep paths below the dam in a couple of inches of water, looking as out of place as a bishop on a manure spreader. Grandfather grazed his sheep on the ball diamond, too. Waste not, want not.

Eagle Park had its home baseball team, which had a reputation for whipping all challengers. Fritz Cassel, who attended the little red schoolhouse and would later serve twenty years in the Ohio legislature, told me that he was the team's water boy. Literally. "Whenever a ball was hit into the pond, I had to go in after it," he said.

Since nearly everyone in the neighborhood was a farmer then, whenever the ice was thick enough, whether it was midweek or weekend, they all stopped work to play hockey. *Weekend* was not a word in our vocabulary. I wonder now, after all these years of so-called progress and prosperity, how many rural neighborhoods have their own free park, kept manicured at a profit by sheep, and the time to enjoy it? When we were poorer, we were a whole lot richer.

The hockey wars shifted to the Pond largely because Dad installed lights that allowed us to follow our madness far into the night without fear of running into burning straw bales. And it continued for a while to serve as a community watering hole as well as a family gathering place, just as Eagle Park had done. The Pond hosted lodge meetings and church groups, although not immersion baptisms as Eagle Park once did, and especially school parties. It's funny how we never thought that those days would end until they did end, and then we hardly realized it until several more years had gone by. One day I looked at my sister and said, almost as if it were a surprise, "You know, we never play hockey at the Pond anymore." The Pond finally became, as so many ponds do when the young people drift away, a forgotten little domain of wild nature where only those with old memories go now and yearn, as James Whitcomb Riley said in his day, to "[s]trip to the soul and dive once more into the old swimmin' hole."

I think the peak year for *Homo hockiatis* on the Pond was 1957 (there was a second peak about 1980), when even in February we were all still eager for one more game. Snow had fallen six inches deep on the ice, however, and a warm wind was melting it and the ice. Uncle Lawrence decided the only way to remove the wet snow quickly was with our Allis Chalmers and its manure scoop. Dad did not think much of the idea, but he went along with it. After all, this probably would be the last game of the season.

Since the tractor had little traction on the ice, Lawrence would start out in the grass, careening along in road gear till he got to the Pond, then drop the blade and let the weight of the tractor slide it and a scoopful of snow to the other bank. Luckily, he had decided to clear the shallow end of the Pond first. Halfway through the job, halfway across the Pond, the thawing February ice gave way, and the tractor sank into four feet of water. Lawrence sat astride the seat, whooping hysterically. "You're still the craziest man I know," Dad yelled at him, shaking his head.

"*Me* crazy?" Lawrence roared with hyenalike laughter. "This is your tractor, not mine!"

A PASTURE POND

When I try to think of the best way to explain my fascination with garden pools and pasture ponds, or in fact any body of water small enough to surround with mind and eye, I think of Claude Monet, one of the greatest of the French impressionist painters. During the last three decades of his life, Monet's oval pond, sixty yards long and twenty yards wide, was almost "the sole source of his inspiration," says his biographer Michael Howard. Monet spent his lifetime trying to capture light on canvas, and when he realized that the best way to do that was to try to paint light on water, he did not have to go beyond his garden to follow his genius. "Once more I have undertaken things which are impossible to do," he wrote in a letter to Gustave Geffroy in 1890. "Water with grasses waving in the depths. . . . It's wonderful to see but it drives you mad to want to do it."

But driven by an impossibility, he went on to produce some of his best-loved paintings: *The Japanese Bridge* in 1899; *The Clouds* in 1903; *Waterlilies* in 1916 and again in 1920—in fact, he painted water lilies dozens of times; *Clouds,* 1914–18; *Green Reflection,* which he worked on for ten years; *The Flowering Arches* in 1912;

and many others. What fascinated him was, in his own words, "the mirror of water whose appearance alters at every moment, thanks to the patches of sky which are reflected in it, and which give it its light and its movement. The passing cloud, the freshening breeze, the storm which threatens and breaks, the wind that blows hard and suddenly abates, the light growing dim and bright again, so many factors undetectable to the uninitiated, which transforms the coloring and disturbs the planes of the water."

Alas, I am not skilled enough to make a living for thirty years writing only about my pasture pond, which lies about two miles from the pond that my father built, and chronologically about forty-five years later. But if I were that clever, thirty years would not be nearly enough time to describe everything that is there to describe. My original purpose in building the pond was much humbler than Monet's. I wanted a swimming hole to jump into and wash off the chaff when I was making hay. That the pond would become a focal point of my attention both as a writer and as a farmer was not at first apparent to me. But I realize in hindsight that what I have built is only incidentally a swimming hole. Because I visit it frequently, it has become a living textbook of ecology that adds new chapters to itself every year. It is a piece of nature's own artwork that changes moods and colors by the hour, and sometimes, as Monet knew, by the second. It is a natural musical instrument that plays different melodies depending on which insects, amphibians, birds, and breezes are in concert. The species of plants and animals that seem to generate spontaneously in the pond, and the life that is drawn to its banks, are, for all practical purposes, unlimited. And I am not counting the uncountable trillions of microscopic plants and animals for which one drop of its water is bigger than the whole pool is to a tadpole and without which the pond would be merely a chemical mixture of hydrogen and oxygen.

I go at least twice a day to the pond, and if I look sharply enough, I will see or smell or hear something new or something that passed through a year ago in its annual cycle and is now returning. Sometimes an event will be so bizarre that I wonder if any other human has ever seen it. One such incident I recorded in an earlier book:

> [A] mating pair of dragonflies fluttered over the water. The female was doing all the flying, while the male, its duty done, I presume, clung stubbornly to its mate's abdomen as it died. The female kept making clumsy, burdened passes over the pond, each time getting closer to the water surface. Finally it dipped down until the dangling male touched water and then *wham!* a striking largemouth bass nipped the male clean away in a quicksilver flash. The female then went merrily on her way, as if she and the largemouth had planned the whole thing. Perhaps they had.

In the pond's planning and construction, I tried to implement all the lessons I had learned in observing or helping build other ponds. I wanted mine small enough to care for easily. On a small pond, I could, for example, pull out a buildup of cattails by hand rather than trying to kill them with chemicals or digging them out with a backhoe.

At the same time the pond had to be practical; poems could come later. I wanted it small enough so that I could state that anyone with a modest income could afford to build one like it. Ours, measuring about fifty feet in diameter, cost us five hundred dollars for a day's work of bulldozer and front-end loader. Yet it had to be big enough to provide at least fifteen meals' total of fish, turtles, frogs, and wetland plants annually. Studying pond manuals, I calculated that a body of water about fifty feet in diameter and six to eight feet deep would be sufficient. After seven years of experience, that calculation still appears achievable, although the pond has not yet reached that level of production. Or rather, we have not harvested everything the pond produces for fear of overharvesting before the pond matures its full complement of life. For instance, we could have taken more in the way of frog legs, cattail rhizomes, and a big fat Canada goose who decided she owned the pond. In the future, as the fish population multiplies, I'm confident that we shall reach the goal of fifteen meals in fish alone, and obtain that many more meals from other water plants and animals. If we need more fish, I will build a second pond, or even a third, of the same size.

There are other advantages to keeping a pond this small. If undesirable fish get in the pond, or desirable ones overpopulate, I can more easily catch them with hook and line or, with the help of other hungry lovers of beer-battered fried fish, seine the pond during dry seasons when the water level is low. Or I can simply pump the water out during the dry season, irrigate the pasture with the nutrient-rich water, save enough fish in a tank for restocking, put the rest in the freezer, and wait for rain to refill the pond.

The pond supplies water for our livestock too. I would like eventually to have a pond in several of our pasture paddocks, so that I can enclose livestock in a particular paddock and not have to carry water to them. In this way the pond or ponds become watery adjuncts to the new grass-farming or pasture-farming system that we are trying to perfect, where grazing animals get most of their food themselves, nearly year-round, without the expense of tractor farming. A pond, viewed in this light, is a water pasture in which water animals "graze" and become high-quality protein food for humans and other animals, with minimal effort or money from the farmer or gardener.

Another reason that small is beautiful in this case is that I wanted to place rocks around the bank and on the floor of the shallow neck end so that our sheep could get to the water for a drink without trampling the banks or muddying the water. My son and I could do this rock work (called rip-rapping) by hand on our small pond and save a lot of money. A stone quarry owner generously allowed us to have all the large flat rocks we wanted for free if we loaded them ourselves on our pickup. Rip-rapping the shoreline from the top of the pond bank down to about three feet in the water was hard work, more than I would have wanted to take on if the pond had been larger.

I had decided that I wanted an excavated pond, a hole in the ground so to speak, rather than an embankment pond requiring the construction of an earthen dam. Artificial dams are expensive and require special flow designs so that water coming into the pond in heavy rain does not overflow the dam and wash it away. On the other hand, I did not want to go to the expense of installing a well and pump out in the middle of the pasture field so we could pump water to fill the pond. That meant that the excavation would have to be filled by runoff rainwater. Furthermore, and this was an absolutely essential condition for the pond, runoff water would have to flow from pasture and/or woodlot or tile drains only. Runoff from cultivated fields could mean that silt, chemicals, and fertilizer would get into the pond.

After I observed the flow of rainwater from our fields for ten years, I realized we had a potentially perfect site for an excavated pond in the pasture right behind the woods. First of all, and most important, I knew the soil here was heavy clay all the way down to China, as we say in Ohio, and would hold water well. Second, rainwater flowed from our neighbor's woodland but from no cultivated field, and from both sides of the pasture into its center and thence on across the field and off our property. In times of heavy rains, this flow route becomes a small stream temporarily—plenty of water to fill a small pond. In fact, there is too much runoff, but because the pond is excavated and does not have a dirt dam, the water can flow into and out of the pond without causing any problems.

I determined the size of the watershed by walking over the area for ten years during heavy spring runoff periods observing the flow of water. Eventually I paced off approximate measurements of this little watershed. An acre is 43,560 square feet, and my typical pace about 2.5 feet. Counting paces and doing the math, I found that the runoff area was approximately six acres, a little more than necessary for my small pond but not too much for an excavated pond to handle.

Then I only had to make sure there was no underground drainage tile close to the pond site. If there had been, I would have rerouted the tile around the pond area, staying at least fifty to one hundred feet away from the site. If it were any closer, the tile might draw water out of the pond by capillary action.

I staked the area where I wanted the pond and decided where to put the excavated soil—into a mound on the westerly side to act as a bit of windbreak. The bulldozer operator, experienced in building ponds, scooped off the top foot of good topsoil from the pond site and made a separate pile of it, which he would later put back on top of the excavated mound of dirt so that grass would grow on it vigorously. Then he dished out the pond hole with his little bulldozer. I wanted a steep bank to discourage pond weeds around the pond's shoreline, and a depth of eight feet at the center. When he would throttle up the steep incline with a blade full of dirt, I had to look away. I thought the 'dozer would surely upend and topple over on its back into the bottom of the hole. My concern amused the operator exceedingly. But watching, or rather not watching, taught me the wisdom of hiring construction work only from businesses that were fully insured, as he was.

We built the pond in the dry season, August here, so as not to be hampered unnecessarily by mud. The pond easily filled by the middle of November. People new to pond building are nearly always surprised by how quickly a pond will fill. A mere inch of water over a six-acre watershed is a lot of water. True to our hopes and reckonings, when the pond was full, the water oozed over the lower side without gouging out a gully even in flooding rains. Because there was only a gentle fall to the field, the water was almost as high on the bank on the upper end of the pond as on the lower, and I had only to rank rocks and fill in dirt about eight inches on the lower end to make the pond equally full on all sides. I left a slot in this row of rocks so that the water overflowed at that outlet and not along the whole bank. Fish generally tend to stay down in deep water during flood times, but if they try to swim out at the outlet in the rocks, they run into a screen (an old barbecue grill) that I have placed there.

The following summer we installed the rock rip-rap around the pond. Generally, on larger ponds, this work is done with a dump truck or a front-end loader, using tons of fist-sized stones. The main purpose of rip-rap is to protect the banks from wave erosion. There was not going to be much wave erosion in so small a pond as ours, but we wanted protection against trampling sheep hooves. As it turned out, our jumble of rocks more or less stairstepped up the bank served another useful function: they gave shelter and protection to minnows. Otherwise, the big fish, great blue herons, turtles, and bullfrogs would have eaten them all before any had a chance to grow to a size we could eat.

Black water beetles, the kind we call whirligigs because they swim round and round on the surface of the water as if they've been enjoying too much Old Grand-Dad, were the first inhabitants of the pond that we noticed. Leopard frogs soon followed. To my surprise, cattails came up almost immediately, indicating that we had situated the pond where a vernal pool must have existed years ago.

In the second year we started stocking the pond with fish. I put in about twenty smallish largemouth bass that we caught in another pond, four hybrid green sunfish, six yellow perch, and four shellcrackers, or redear sunfish, which have a preference for snails and so keep them from overpopulating. Both kinds of sunfish afford table fare as delicious as their cousin, the bluegill. Perch are not always recommended in warm-water farm ponds such as ours, but I learned from the Amish that they do just fine in ponds, and I think they are the best-tasting fish of all, even better than trout. We could not raise trout, although I would have liked to. They require cool springwater (fifty to fifty-five degrees Fahrenheit) and won't thrive in a warmwater pond like ours.

The Fish and Wildlife Service and the Soil Conservation Service have reams of information and recommendations for stocking farm ponds, and these recommendations are repeated commonly in pond manuals. Fish can't read manuals and are just as obstinate and unpredictable as humans when it comes to sex. In my experience an overpopulation of something will occur in your pond no matter how finely you calculate your ratios of predator fish to prey fish. The experts usually recommend bluegills and largemouth bass as the mainstays of a warm-water farm pond, because they thrive in this environment and both are good to eat. Then the experts go to considerable trouble to determine what ratio of bluegills to bass to stock (I believe three bluegills to one bass is currently the most favored number, but not by me). The idea is to stock enough bluegills so that the bass have plenty to eat, but not so many that the bluegill population explodes. I think it is better to stock about an even number of both or, if you aren't going to fish hard for bluegills, three times as many bass as bluegills or other sunfish.

Largemouth bass are the tigers of the pond world. They eat all small fish (including their own fry), frogs, and salamanders. They eat insects and snakes. They will even eat small mammals and have been known to come right out of the water and nab low-flying birds. Bluegills, like all the sunfish family, live mostly on the insect life of the pond, which in turn feeds on plankton. Bluegills love fishworms and leeches and usually will adapt to eating milled grains and bread crumbs. They do not eat minnows normally, and so they work well with largemouth bass, which eat minnows mainly.

But it is almost impossible to assure a stable balance between the two species or any other species in any given pond, no matter what ratio you start with, because population dynamics are so complex. Not only will the bass eat their own young as well as the sunfish minnows, but there are many other predators that must be taken into account: humans and how regularly they fish the pond, and particularly what size fish they take; bullfrogs; herons; turtles; raccoons; opossums; kingfishers; mink; and increasingly in our area, bald eagles, cormorants, and ospreys.

In our small pond I can count the fish almost as I count the sheep in our flock. That is the only sure way I know to manage fish populations. If something is getting the upper hand, we can catch and eat the surplus species and toss the other species back in. Right now bullfrogs are overpopulating, and because they are voracious predators of minnows and other frogs, we should harvest a dinner of frog legs soon.

You can count fish accurately only when the water is clear, of course, and much ado is made in fish manuals about clarifying the water. We do nothing, but in the fall and winter, and after summer rains—except when we are wading enough to stir up the thin film of slime that always rests on the floor of the pond or when runoff is flowing into the pond—the water is crystal clear. Count fish at these times. In spring and early summer, the water clouds as the microscopic animal and plant life burgeons. Often in the growing season there will be a scum of air-sifted seeds, pollen, chaff, or algae on the surface of the pond that makes the water look dirty. Wind or mechanical agitation will push the scum away, revealing limpid water. If our pond started to appear muddy all the time, I'd know that muskrats or Canada geese had invaded it or that the livestock had decided to go wading. The latter situation is not likely, because the sheep are afraid of water and our cow is fearful of slipping on the rocks around the pond. If muskrats take up residence, we can eat them. I've not tried that yet but am told that, being entirely vegetarian in diet, muskrats are quite tasty and safe to eat.

I try to keep at least two large largemouth bass in the pond at all times to feed on the sunfish that have grown past the size a smaller largemouth can handle. The biggest ones usually get to the hook first, and so often I release them back to the water, making sure I wet my hands before taking them off the hook. A dry hand can pull off the protective mucus on the fish's skin. When I fish for these half-tame, eager eaters, I dangle the baited hook just at the surface of the water and try to keep it moving. This way the fish usually strike and get hooked only in the lip and can be released with little or no harm. If the fish swallows the hook, grasp the middle of the fish firmly between thumb and fingers right behind the pectoral fins, cupping the palm of your hand over the dorsal spines in such a way that you don't get poked by them. Then with the index finger of your other hand, follow the fish line down in the fish's gullet until you locate the hook (you may be able to see it). Stick the tip of your index finger down the fish's throat until it rests inside the curve of the hook behind the barb. Then gently *back* the hook out of the flesh, which usually means pushing it farther down into the fish's gullet. Often this can be accomplished with only minor injury to the fish. With your finger securely inside the curve of the hook, you can then gingerly guide it back out of the fish's mouth without rehooking it or yourself. If you can't get the hook out without considerable injury to the fish, keep the fish for eating rather than releasing it back to the pond, because there's a good chance it will die anyway.

There are fish traps that can be set on the pond floor or suspended in the water. Sometimes they work. You can get these (and all other pond equipment imaginable) by studying the ads in a magazine called *Farm Pond Harvest,* which is particularly tailored to the recreational user of farm ponds. Other magazines and manuals I am familiar with focus on commercial fish-production methods and are not as useful for owners of small ponds or garden pools.

After several years of growing fish in the little pasture pond, we have experienced the best production from the largemouth bass, which is not surprising since that is what we stocked the most. We held our first harvest two years after introduction. Our grandsons caught fifteen bass in about fifteen minutes, because the fish are almost tame and accustomed to eating worms that we feed them occasionally. The boys now think all fishing should be like that! The next year we caught another batch. We did not take any out last year, because extremely dry weather kept the pond low—below the rip-rap—and the big fish ate all the new fry, which had no place to hide. Since we depend on the new fry to increase the "flock," it seemed best to skip a harvest. Last year, with plenty of rain, the pond stayed more or less full, and in September there were half a zillion tiny minnows. I concluded that we were on our way to a stable supply of fifteen meals' worth every year. Time will tell.

The hybrid green sunfish, which, like mules, are not supposed to propagate, and the redear sunfish have grown only very slowly but are now big enough to eat, if I wanted to catch them. They seem to be doing a good job of keeping snails from overpopulating, and I have not seen any leeches, so I shall not catch any of them yet.

The original perch disappeared. I found one beheaded on the bank. Our cat may have caught it (he is fascinated with the fish), but more than likely it was a raccoon, since footprints of this fish fancier are always in evidence around the pond. Or maybe it was the coyote that I have seen napping on the rip-rap. I don't know that coyotes can catch fish but believe they are smart enough. One sunfish escaped in high water when the screen over the outlet fell into the pond. I found it half eaten too. I don't know what happened to the other perch. I thought they were large enough that the bass could not eat them, but now I think I was wrong. This year I added eight more small perch, and they too disappeared. If the largemouth bass are not the culprit, perhaps the great blue heron caught them. At any rate, I will now stock four *big* perch.

None of our fish grow as fast as I would like, yet. They won't eat commercial fish food, which would solve that problem. I have asked professional aquaculturists about this. They say that fish hatched and raised in completely artificial pools grow accustomed to eating commercial food from the start because that's all they have available. They will continue to eat commercial food if transferred to a wilder environment, like a natural pond. They will then "teach" their offspring and other fish to eat that food. If my more or less wild fish don't eat commercial feed, it is because they have never had any and are getting enough to eat in the form of minnows, bugs, and worms. Needless to say, the advisor who was selling commercial feed said I could train my fish to eat the stuff, and the other advisor, who sold natural food (minnows) for fish, doubted if I could. Oh well. I will stick with natural food. I accept slower growth rates as part of my pond philosophy: the pond should be a self-contained, self-sustainable, biological "machine" fueled only by solar energy.

Though our pond is still too young to have reached its full potential in aquatic life, if indeed that is possible, its species diversity is mounting rapidly. Along with the patch of cattails that came up naturally, I started some yellow pond lilies I found growing in our creek. Both give shade and protection to the fish and amphibians while adding oxygen to the water. The yellow water lilies are not showy like other water lilies and would be a mistake in a large pond because they tend to spread rapidly. But they are very hardy and well acclimated to this area. I simply pulled pieces of root from the ones growing in our creek, and they readily rooted. When they get too rowdy, I merely pull some of them out.

In spring I put an old Christmas tree or two in the water, too, to protect fish eggs and spawning minnows from predators. Later in summer I remove the trees. Some fish, especially the perch, so the books say, will lay their gelatinous strings of eggs among the branches, where they are somewhat safer from ducks and other predators. The painted turtles love to climb on the Christmas trees, and I have a hunch they eat some of the fish and frog eggs too.

Waterweeds, plankton, and algae add oxygen to the water and offer protection and food to minnows, tadpoles, and water insects, but they tend to get out of hand. When an overabundance of algae dies, it rots and robs oxygen from the water, possibly inducing a fish kill. For a few years I weeded by hand, scooping out the algae with a pitchfork.

Then I learned about the triploid strain of white amur, or grass carp, which are legal in ponds now because they have been rendered sterile by genetic manipulation. The fertilized eggs are submitted to high barometric pressure, after which, when the cell divides, one of the two new cells is triploid and functionally sterile. The other dies. These fish proved to be excellent pond weeders. In fact, they are one of the few examples of really effective biological weed control that I have observed. They will eat just about everything that grows in our pond except the water lilies. Learning their dislike for the lilies, we now plan to put the showier kinds in the pond in pots so they can't spread and can be lifted out in winter.

The grass carp ate the bottom-rooted water plants first. Then they ate most of the floating algae. After that, they started in on the cattails, a feat we found astounding. They rooted around the cattail roots like pigs on pasture, eating the rhizomes, which I know from experience are good human food too. Lacking anything else to eat, they then pulled the stalks down into the water and gnawed away. I had to put a wire fence around a little section of the cattails to save them. In seasons when there aren't many plants for the white amur to eat, I toss handfuls of grass into the pond. When I mow around the pond, the carp wait for clipped blades of grass to fly into the water. In China, where white amur and other carp are raised commercially, aquaculturists joke that the fish will crawl up on shore when they get hungry, graze awhile, and then jump back in the water.

The Division of Wildlife in Ohio advises stocking white amur at the rate of five per acre if 20–40 percent of the pond is covered with algae, ten per acre if algae cover 40–60 percent of the pond, and twenty if algal cover is over 60 percent. Obviously a very small pond like ours would take only one or two. After two years with two grass carp growing to the three-pound size, I began to worry that they were not leaving enough plant life to keep the water oxygenated. One would have been enough, it seemed. But how do you catch a grass carp easily? I was told they eat only plants and are not interested in anything I could put on a hook. We had just about decided to shoot one of them with the bow and arrow, with heavy fish line tied to the arrow shaft. But on a warm day in February, my grandsons persuaded me to go fishing. Okay. We could catch a couple of bass, maybe, although they usually don't bite much that early in the year. We settled ourselves on the pond bank. I worked a worm on the hook and cast into the pond, preparing to hand the pole over to Grandson No. 1. Wham! The cork disappeared, and I found myself almost pulled into the icy water. No bass in our pond was big enough yet to fight like that. Sure enough, I had caught one of the grass carp. I guess it hadn't read the book that says grass carp are vegetarians. I now understand from other water watchers that grass carp will eat not only worms but fish eggs and for that reason may not be desirable in a small pond. Enough minnows seem to be surviving to feed the other fish and increase the flock, so I'll keep my one grass carp for the wonderful job it does of preventing algae from overwhelming the pond.

My wife, Carol, baked the other grass carp for dinner that night, and Pawpaw, Daddy, and grandsons prepared to enjoy what the books say is a much tastier kind of carp than the common Egyptian carp. It was okay but not really to my liking, no matter what aquaculture books say or how much catsup I put on it. (I have been told, since then, that all carp need to spend twenty-four hours in a bucket or tank of clean water before being killed and butchered. In this way the flesh loses its muddy taste. Well, maybe so.) If you cure this carp with salt and then hickory smoke it, as I have with regular carp, and drink a beer with the salty morsels, I suppose the taste would be improved but probably not your health. Otherwise, well, I believe bass and sunfish are much better and perch a hundred million times better.

Nevertheless, the one remaining grass carp did not keep the weeds and algae down well enough to suit me, so I have added a second, small one. A big one and a small one equals one and a half grass carp, which is evidently right for a pond the size of ours.

If you like catfish, channel cats are a good species for ponds, since they generally won't overpopulate as other catfish will in a warm-water pond. That's what the manuals say, anyway. I believe nothing in books about fish anymore unless I have verified it on my own. I won't put catfish in my pond for the simple reason that I prefer to eat bass, sunfish, and perch. Also, except for the grass carp, I *want* the species I raise to increase and multiply.

If the grass carp were not as tasty as I expected, the largemouth bass have been simply delicious, coming out of clean pond water, kept on ice, and fileted and fried in cornmeal within an hour or two after catching. The cornmeal is fresh-shelled from a cob of our open-pollinated corn and beer-battered. Largemouth bass are not deemed by gourmets to be as tasty as bluegills, perch, or trout. I think that all four, fresh from a pond, are manna from heaven. But you need to filet them; they have lots of tiny bones.

Painted turtles arrived in the pond soon after the leopard frogs and the green frogs. There must be some telecommunication system in the wild. The word gets around. Hey. New water in Logsdon's sheep pasture. To my disappointment, I have seen only one water snake visit the pond so far, and it disappeared. I've tried adding a couple of crayfish from the creek, but the bass nailed them right away. Beware of stocking crayfish (or crawdads, as we call them). Nonnative types reportedly overpopulate quickly and, because they are also good for-agers, will clean a pool of plant and animal life that more desirable species require. I do not think our crawdads, from the creek nearby, will cause a problem, and of course crawdad tails taste quite a bit like lobster tails, though they are much smaller. I just haven't gotten around to stocking any more.

Once I put a bluntnose minnow from the creek in the pond. A bass gave chase immediately. The poor little minnow launched itself completely out of the water in trying to escape, and when it came back down, the bass was there to swallow it. So far I have not seen a snapping turtle in the pond but am sure some will come when the proper food supply occurs. Snapper meat is a great delicacy.

Plant life in the pond is more varied than animal life. Each species has its characteristic place: emergent weeds like cattails, water lilies, and bulrushes in the shallower water; submerged weeds like pond-weed, coontail, and water milfoil around the shoreline; algae of various kinds drifting in the water; and microscopic plankton throughout, which, like the others, add oxygen to the water. I have not even tried to identify all the water plants that seem so mysteriously to find the pond. My mind is not big enough to keep track of all of nature's ways on even this one small pond, let alone our small farm. If a plant grows up and sports gold coins, I'll probably learn its name. I'll even learn its Latin name.

I didn't equip the pond with a mechanical agitator or circulator to add more oxygen to the water, again because of my determination to manage a pond on solar energy alone. But there are wind-powered agitators, which my philosophy would allow, that would be practical on larger ponds. The problem is that when oxygen supply is critical, it is often on a hot day when there is no wind.

For our fish the oxygen is supplied by the wind rippling the surface water, by falling and inflowing rainwater, and by water plants breathing in carbon dioxide and giving off oxygen. That means we can keep only as many fish as can exist in the pond without supplemental oxygen. So far, so good. Every year in the hottest part of summer, when water level is lowest, I expect to go to the pond and find fish swimming on the surface, gulping air. If that happens, I will get some kind of motorized agitator to stir up the water. A little trolling-boat motor would work fine. Or I will catch a lot of fish in a hurry for eating. But oxygen shortage hasn't happened yet, and I don't think it will.

Once in the middle of winter, when I was clearing snow off the ice so sunlight could get through and stimulate microscopic plant growth and therefore oxygen generation, I said to myself, "But there are no plants this time of year to generate oxygen, are there?" So I rigged up a pole with a plastic dipper on the end of it, chopped a hole in the ice, and dipped some water off the pond bottom. I poured the water in a jar and set the jar on the windowsill in the house. There were fine hairs in the water that, in the warmth of the house, began to grow quite vigorously. Algae! Under a microscope, all sorts of little animals and plants that were invisible to the naked eye were careening around in the water. There was life in the pond in the dead of January.

It appears that my fish hibernate in the mud at the bottom of the pond during winter. I have never read about this phenomenon. But in the winter after a hard drought, the water was less than four feet deep at the center of the pond and crystal clear. I could easily see the bottom everywhere in the pond. No fish! I thought that something had eaten them all, but that seemed highly unlikely. The fish remained out of sight all winter, and I was mystified. When thaw time and slightly warmish weather came, there they were again. There was only one possible conclusion. The bass, sunfish, and grass carp had snuggled down in the debris on the pond bottom and hibernated. Sure enough, I finally found corroboration in books. Some fish, sometimes, do hibernate or achieve some state of half-sleep akin to hibernation.

That experience also seemed to demonstrate that the requirement here in the North that fish have six to eight feet of water for survival over winter is not necessarily true. That winter the ice froze about five inches, under which there was barely three feet of water for a month—until February, when the snow melted and the pond filled again. There were no dead fish.

Other ponds familiar to me regularly suffer thermal inversion of the water in summer. This turnover occurs when the water in the bottom layer of the pond, which has much less oxygen in it in a deep pond and is much cooler, rises to the surface. This happens when the surface water cools to the temperature of the bottom water in the fall or spring or after a summer rainstorm. The oxygen level in the mixed waters falls drastically, which can cause a massive fish kill. Mechanical circulation systems can keep stratification and therefore inversions from happening by constantly recirculating bottom water to the top. With our pond averaging hardly six feet deep and sometimes less in summer, and with a good flow of fresh water entering during rainy spring and late fall seasons, there has not been a noticeable stratification problem so far. In such a small pond, swimming stirs up the water about as well as a mechanical circulator or agitator.

Our pond supports at least five kinds of dragonflies, all of which eat other insects, including mosquitoes. They are streamlined, often colorful fliers. The stock lestes, a damselfly I usually see in the pasture near the pond, has a metallic green abdomen with tiny black and white bands; a thorax shiny green on top, yellowish on the bottom; a bulbous blue eye; and a yellow-and-black design on the back of the prothorax that looks like a tiny monkey face. If this insect were as big as even the smallest bird, its striking beauty would be a subject of poems and art. But I doubt that one person in ten thousand knows about it. The bright red dragonfly I see frequently must be a half-banded toper, although this species is supposed to be rare. The green darner is sometimes blue; the white-tail and the twelve-spotted skimmers are rakishly black and white. I can't yet tell the bluets from the short-stalked damselfly. All of them can fly swifter than any bird.

Once, while walking near the pond on a hot evening in August, I saw a strange sight: several kinds of dragonflies, reflecting blue, green, and gold coloration in the sunset, were winging round and round in a sort of loose swarm over a particular spot of the pasture. They did not disperse as I stepped among them, but even at very close range I could not tell why they were flying rather frantically over just this one location. Every few seconds, I could hear a barely discernible snapping noise. I sat down to watch. The dragonflies continued to circle around me, paying no attention to my presence as far as I could tell, which is unusual for dragonflies. The setting sun was almost on the horizon before I could discern what they were doing. In the low light I began to notice other insects, tinier than gnats, rising from the ground around me. So tiny were they, in fact, that I could not see them until they were airborne and the sunlight struck them at a certain angle. They were ascending straight into the air. None of them that I could notice ever got beyond ten feet up before being snatched by a dragonfly. Every snatch was accompanied by that faint, eerie, snapping sound. I could not identify the prey or the several species of dragonfly involved. I wonder if anyone else has ever witnessed so odd a scene.

Toads are the most productive of the creatures that use our pond. They come by the score in the first warm days of spring and begin their singing and mating. Their actions are slightly gross in an orgasmic manner of speaking—pond pornography. After mating they fling and sling their jellylike strings of eggs all over the pond in reckless disarray. Before the eggs hatch, the adults disappear, going back to wherever they spend the rest of the year, mostly in the woods nearby and in our fields and gardens. Soon the water around the edges of the pond turns black with tadpoles, a seemingly limitless feast for fish and other aquatic animals and birds. In a couple of weeks, tiny legs appear on the tadpoles, and as the legs grow, the tails drop off.

Why does nature go to so much trouble? Why not keep it simple, with water animals distinct from land animals, and no amphibians partaking of both kinds of life? I believe watching tadpoles grow from water animals to land animals is an annual replaying of the eons-long process of evolution, every century becoming a millisecond in the early life of a toad. The tiny toadlets, no larger than crickets and easily mistaken for bugs, crawl out of the water in about a month and disappear into the pasture grass. Many of them are eaten at this time. All summer the little toads hop over pasture and lawn, some eaten by predators, some getting killed by mowing, but a few surviving. They grow to the size of walnuts by fall, dig into the ground, and emerge the following spring for the annual trek to the pond, reminding me of college kids flocking to Florida for spring break.

But there are always problems, mostly because of human behavior. This summer a distraught garden-pool owner called to say that she was witnessing a plague of toads. She didn't mind particularly, but the neighbors were complaining about the number of toads their lawn-mowers were mangling. I told her that the problem could be mostly solved by setting the mower blade to cut at three inches above the ground instead of lower. Most of the toads simply flatten out as the mower passes over them and are not hurt. But of course, humans often insist that their lawns look like a rug, and not a shag rug either.

I have not seen blue-spotted black salamanders at the pond yet. They are around; we find them in the garden, especially in the moist, deep mulch under the strawberry plants. That means that, somewhere in our vicinity, they are collecting in still water very early in the spring, when the weather is still relatively cold, for their annual mating game. They may be congregating in the vernal pool in the woods near the pond when we have presumed that it was too early and cold for sexual hi-liggety. Discovering where they go to mate is another adventure in water watching that still awaits us.

Canada geese and several kinds of ducks stop at the pond every spring, checking it out for possible nesting sites. I definitely do not want a congregation of geese on our tiny pond, as they would muddy the banks and manure the water too much, but for a few mornings I can walk out to the pond and carry on a silent conversation with a pair of these awesome birds. My daily appearance is enough to persuade them to move on, to other ponds that humans do not frequent as often. The ducks, mallards mostly, shift to the creek to raise their families. I have erected a wood-duck nest in the pond in the hope of luring this most beautiful of all birds.

To appreciate the full worth of a pasture pond, I visualize it as part of the extended environment of the farm, which—with the creek running through the lower pastures, the two vernal pools in the upper and lower woods, and the second pond I hope to build between the first one and the creek—becomes the watery balance to the meadows and woods. Such a farm can only continue to increase in self-sustaining animal and plant species, powered and operated almost totally by the sun. Here is all the paradise I desire, all the paradise I need.

A MODERN THOREAU
BESIDE A MODERN WALDEN POND

Imagine Thoreau as a master craftsman, forging his thoughts in steel rather than writing them on paper. Imagine that instead of just living beside Walden Pond, he actually built Walden Pond. Imagine further that instead of constructing a rude hut for a two-year hiatus beside Walden Pond, he built a comfortable log house there from scratch and lives in it permanently. Now, if you have any imagination left, imagine that instead of being able to depend if necessary on financial support from the family factory in Concord, *this* Thoreau, with his father at his side, built his own factory next to his own Walden Pond and makes a living from it.

Meet Danny Downs.

Meet his father, Paul Downs.

Paul and Danny (how often in their neighborhood you hear it pronounced Paulandanny!) don't live out in the rural countryside, as you might assume from their homestead of woodland, pond, orchard, market garden, bee yard, and barn full of metal- and woodworking equipment, but in the outer suburbs of a large city. I'm not going to say which one, because I fear their remarkable ways would draw publicity enough to disrupt their lives.

Paul Downs has seen great changes in his seventy years. He still works ancestral land, a remnant of what is left of the farm where he and his siblings grew up, now mostly covered with suburban homes except in the steep hollows where the cows used to pasture. He remembers making hay and driving tractors and picking blackberries and going on horse-drawn sleigh rides where the houses now stand. In those days he would "never never ever" have believed what was going to happen. He watched the farm disappear little by little: the log cabin in the woods where his parents first lived; the granary that they next turned into a house, where he was born; the barn where he worked in younger years; the silo he helped build; and finally the fields too. Even the creek he played beside as a boy disappeared. The city put a sewer line through the hollow between the new houses and sucked the creek into the bowels of the earth. "There is nothing sacred anymore except money," Paul says. There are tears in his eyes. Like any seventy-year-old seeing his own life disappearing, Paul is never far from tears these days.

Most people with deep love of the land would have moved away to live where the world would not remind them every waking hour of what has disappeared. But Paul, a sociable person, embraced the suburb as it embraced him and built his house right next to it. In his spare time he grew vegetables and fruit on his remnant of farm and sold them to the newcomers. He learned not only to tolerate his neighbors but to like them. And they all came to love him and his family and his big garden.

But I'm ahead of my story. His job, after a stint in the air force, was as an air traffic controller. For a while he drove a hundred miles back home when he was off work to help his father on the farm. By and by he got transferred to his home city, and by and by the farm turned into houses, and by and by, out of his love for farming, he gradually turned the few acres of land he had kept out of the old farm into a tidy little homestead where he and his wife, Anne, brought up their three children and pretended that the old ways were not passing away.

All three of Paul and Anne's children turned out to be remarkably talented. Their daughter, Diane, as a schoolteacher, developed such an effective way to teach music to little children that she is now invited all over the nation to share with teachers and famous musicians her unique methods. Paul Jr. is a high school band director who builds model trains so skillfully that his work has attracted journalistic attention. Danny, the third and youngest child, exhibited from his earliest years not only the Downs family ability to master practical skills, but the singularly independent spirit that his ancestors brought down out of the Kentucky mountains with them several generations earlier. (His grandfather was fond of telling about an uncle and aunt who lived quite comfortably on a small hill farm without any visible source of cash income and boasted that they struck only one match a year, to start the fire in the fireplace in the fall.)

Danny's independence made him a difficult child to bring up in a modern world. In his mid-thirties now, he laughs when I suggest that. He would rather talk about his work, not his private life, but decides to make an exception. "I got kicked out of grade school. In fact, I made it my goal to get kicked out. I hated the regimentation. It was a private school with uniforms and all that. I couldn't stand it. I felt like I couldn't breathe. So I misbehaved until they had to throw me out." He says it as if that were an accomplishment to be admired. Since I hated school too, I admire. "I didn't do well in the public school, either," he continues. "But I realized by then that my family was going to insist that I go to some kind of school no matter what, so I cooperated enough to get through it."

Although Danny seemed not to be able to handle conventional classroom subjects, he knew, and so did his parents, that he was far from being a slow learner. He says that he was deemed dyslexic, "but I could read books that interested me just fine." That he excelled at practical skills did not at first impress the family, because most of them excelled that way too. Paul is an excellent furniture maker and house builder. He added to his home a large family room with a fireplace and a large master bedroom that are better built than the original house, and then filled them with his own handcrafted furniture. All of Paul's brothers are accomplished in various practical arts, too. When I asked Anne what she did to encourage her children to carry the tradition to new heights, she shrugged. "When they would ask me how to do something, I'd tell them to figure it out for themselves. And they did. If you ask Diane how her schoolchildren learn to play music together so well in her percussion ensembles without knowing how to read music, she will tell you she has no idea. No one told her how to teach music effectively to little children. She invented her own way. She thinks that because she was dyslexic, she learned to communicate with children better in verbal ways outside the normal teaching regime."

Were Anne and Paul worried about Danny's uncooperative spirit in school? "Well, yes, we thought Danny should get a regular education," Anne says, "but after a while I could see that wasn't going to work. Once I took Danny to a school that offered courses in blacksmithing. We listened to the school official telling us about the school's practical arts program, but he did not mention blacksmithing. Danny asked why. 'Well, that comes in the second year. You have to take these regular college courses first.' Danny got up. 'Come on, Mom. We're going home.'"

It was not a laughing matter at the time, but Paul chuckles now. "I've come around to Danny's way of looking at this. If you want to read Shakespeare, fine, but if you don't want to read Shakespeare, that's fine too. By what right do schools dictate to others their notion of what's important in a curriculum?"

If I wished a boy to know something about the arts and sciences, for instance, I would not pursue the common course, which is merely to send him into the neighborhood of some professor, where anything is professed and practiced but the art of life. Which would have advanced the most at the end of a month—the boy who had made his own jack-knife from the ore which he had dug and smelted . . . or the boy who had attended the lectures on metallurgy at the Institute and had received a penknife from his father? Which would be most likely to cut his fingers? (Thoreau, *Walden*)

I thought of my friend David Kline, a writer of fine books and nature essays who has only a grade school education (and who also has a fine pond). "So what did you do with Danny then?" I asked.

"I guess the first time I realized that Danny was maybe unusual was on a vacation trip to the folk museum at Williamsburg, Virginia," recalls Paul. "When we stopped at the blacksmith shop, Danny was, like, transfixed. He was just fourteen. He spent the entire time we were there at that forge, watching the blacksmith work. Back home he built a little hand forge out of an old tire rim, sort of like what farmers made and used when I was a boy. He just went right at it, and the more he learned about metalworking, the less he learned in school."

The mode of founding a college is commonly to get up a subscription of dollars and cents, and then following blindly the principles of a division of labor to its extreme . . . to call in a contractor . . . and he employs . . . operatives actually to lay the foundations, while the students that are to be [educated there] are said to be fitting themselves for it. . . . I think that it would be better . . . for the students . . . to lay the foundation up themselves. (Thoreau, *Walden*)

Paul continues. "I decided I had to get involved personally, not just with words, but with action. The first thing we did was build a workshop. We built it to look like a barn and big enough, we thought, for both my woodworking tools and his metalworking equipment. We worked a lot together after that, he at his forge and

I at my woodworking. Even then he was uncommonly particular. I'm pretty particular myself, but he was forever finding fault with my work. In machining metal, a fraction of a millimeter makes a difference, and early on, Danny understood that. No tolerance. And he doesn't much tolerate *anything* that interferes with his work, either."

Danny needed metalworking tools that, if available at all, would cost a fortune at today's prices. He learned how to find what he wanted in junkyards or abandoned in dusty corners of warehouses and factories or at industrial machinery sales. He'd buy or beg some hulking wreck of metal and restore it to working condition. For example, the huge trip-hammer that he uses almost daily was made in 1915. It cost him $650 at a sale, plus $150 to put it on his truck to haul home. An equivalent trip-hammer, new, costs $90,000, Danny says. He has many uses for the trip-hammer, among them occasionally making railroad lock rods, a job that pays him $200 an hour. "Not bad for late-eighteenth-century technology," he says, smiling. With similar deals he has now filled the barn with enough machinery to do just about anything that can be done with iron and steel, and a lot with copper, brass, and aluminum, while Paul's woodworking tools retreat farther into one corner of the barn.

"Once I understood that the knowledge and tools were out there to make almost *anything,* it filled me with—oh, I don't know how to express it—a kind of fascination and wonder," Danny says. "I began to care a lot more about making things than about making money. A pile of junk iron available for free can be transformed into all kinds of useful tools and things. And there's all the stuff you can make out of wood. It is totally amazing to me how much potentially valuable metal and wood is simply thrown away every day. And look at all the food you can grow for yourself. If you have knowledge, you don't need much money."

The ways by which you get money almost without exception lead downward. To have done anything merely to make money is to have been truly idle or worse. If the laborer gets no more than the wages which the employer pays him, he is cheated, he cheats himself. (Thoreau, *Walden*)

Danny began to exhibit extraordinary talent. He taught himself how to make Damascus steel, an art that was commonly practiced in the days when there were more swords than pistols but has been all but forgotten today in America. He built a model of a Stirling hot-air engine that actually works. Robert Stirling invented his engine in 1837 as an improvement on the steam engine because, being driven by hot air, not steam, it is lighter and safer. Stirling engines are now being tried on rockets and space shuttles to generate power from solar heat. Danny's model not only works but is a work of art. He made it out of scraps of metal around his shop. Out of such scraps he also makes "obsolete" forging tools he can't find anywhere. He built from scratch, and mostly junk, a band-saw mill to saw boards from dead or dying trees he cuts in the woods or wherever he can scrounge them. He built a drying shed to store the lumber in. He rebuilt the old family farm tractor so that it will run for another fifty years. He built a woodshed near his house to hold the wood he burns in the fireplace and for cooking down maple syrup that he and Paul collect—in an evaporator he also built.

> Every man looks at his wood-pile with a kind of affection. I love to have mine before my window, and the more chips the better to remind me of my pleasing work. (Thoreau, *Walden*)

Meanwhile, Paul was establishing the orchard and gardens next to the barn. Danny invited a beekeeper, looking for a place to keep her bees, to put hives in the orchard. He was fascinated by the bees. He soon started his own hives and now is selling or giving away his own honey. When Paul added rooms to their house, Danny watched and decided that, with Dad's help, he could build himself a house too. The construction, started when Danny was seventeen, took them several years of slow, painstaking work because they scrounged and retrofitted material, or built from scratch. Like Thoreau, Danny felled trees in the woods and hewed them flat on two sides by hand for his walls, having not yet built the band-saw mill he now uses. When he couldn't find an old hewing ax that suited him, he made one. He and Paul laid up the magnificent fireplace and chimney with creek-bed rocks that they hauled up out of the hollows.

> When I came to build my chimney, I studied masonry. My bricks, being second-hand ones, required to be cleaned with a trowel, so that I learned more than usual of the qualities of bricks. . . . I picked out as many fireplace bricks as I could find . . . and filled the places between the bricks . . . with stones from the pond shore, and also made my mortar with the white sand from the same place. (Thoreau, *Walden*)

Today if I stand with my back to the suburban houses and look at Danny's house, what I see could be a little homestead out of the past, except for the pickup truck in the lane. Not in my most fanciful mood could I write a make-believe story more unusual than the reality Paulandanny have created.

> I learned this, at least, by my experiment [of living at Walden]: that if one advances confidently in the direction of his dreams, and endeavors to live the life which he has imagined, he will meet with a success unexpected in common hours. . . . In proportion as he simplifies his life, the laws of the universe will appear less complex and solitude will not be solitude, nor weakness weakness. If you have built castles in the air, your work need not be lost; that is where they should be. Now put the foundations under them. (Thoreau, *Walden*)

Metalworking contracts began coming to Danny from builders, from factories, from homeowners. Once a metallurgist from an aerospace engineering firm called him. The company wanted some tongs made to use in forging out test bars for a project involving airplane tie-downs for a navy aircraft carrier. Danny told him he could make the tongs and also forge the test bars, which needed to be very, very precise—.615 of an inch diameter and about 12 feet long. The metallurgist soon called back. He was intrigued. He wanted to bring his top shop foreman and learn how Danny would do what he said he could do. "I tried to discourage him," Danny says. "Those guys work in white lab coats in state-of-the-art facilities with sparkling floors and lots of people around to do the work. I told them I worked out in a barn in the middle of a field and most of my equipment was nearly a hundred years old."

The metallurgist and the shop foreman came anyway, flying in from several states away. The heat on the test bars was critical, needing to be above 1,900 degrees Fahrenheit, they told Danny. They had brought along a digital pyrometer to check the heat. It was broken, so Danny fixed it for them, even though he knew he didn't need it. He just watched the color of the metal in the forge until he announced that it was above 1,900 degrees. In disbelief the visitors checked it with their pyrometer. The temperature was 1,950 degrees. "They were amazed. They stayed four days, watching me work," Danny recalls. "I made a swage and hammered out the test bars to the required .615 inch plus or minus .003, the thickness of a sheet of paper. They could hardly believe what they were seeing. I kept thinking that these guys did work for NASA and the military, and here they were, totally fascinated, in a blacksmith shop that could double as an antique tool museum."

Nowadays, the boy who almost flunked out of school, who was thought therefore to be doomed to a lowly, second-rate life, averages about forty dollars an hour at jobs he could often charge more for because few people know how to do them. Money does not matter that much to him. He is content to make a moderate living while reserving plenty of time for increasing his quality of life in nonmonetary ways.

For example, he is a friend of a man with cerebral palsy who can't talk or use his hands, who could not even urinate without help. His friend had an idea for equipping his wheelchair with a urinal and wondered if Danny could engineer it. Of course. "It took more than a little doing, but it worked," says Danny. "For the first time in his thirty-six years, my friend could take a leak by himself."

Danny designed other changes to make the wheelchair easier to operate. The day I visited him in his workshop, he was repairing a delicate piece of mechanism from the chair control that had to fit perfectly, a repair that most shops would not be able to do or for which they would have to charge a lot of money. Danny charged nothing. He is not even interested in trying to patent his urinal, although surely someone will and will make a bunch of money. To Danny there are better things to do in life than make a bunch of money.

A spring gurgles out of the hillside near Danny's log house and workshop. He and his father have eyed it speculatively for years. Recently Danny decided to harness it as a source of water for a fishing and swimming pond. "Paulandanny" went to work. There was a problem that seemed to preclude a pond in this location. This is sinkhole country, where you can pour water down a hole in the ground forever and not raise a puddle. With a backhoe they dug out an excavation about forty-five feet by ninety feet and six feet deep just downhill from the spring. Then they picked up rocks off the pond bed and smoothed it out with a harrow and tractor. Next, they laid down a layer of geotextile felt, about an eighth of an inch in thickness, and on top of that a thirty-mil plastic liner that the supplier made to size by heat-gluing together the edges of several rolls. Another layer of the felt went over the plastic. The felt protects the liner from accidental gouging. The felt cost four hundred dollars, the liner eleven hundred. "The liner weighed 650 pounds and was difficult for Dad and me to unroll over the pond bed," says Danny. "It also took some time to smooth out all the folds in the liner." On top of the liner they spread a mixture of pea gravel and sand about six inches deep. Around the edge of the pond they ranked rocks, tucking the liner under them. To get the rocks even all around and at the right height, Danny used a transit level, set it at the planned water level, and then marked the pond bank on all sides.

They graded the land above the pond so that only springwater could get into it and hardly any runoff water. That meant they did not have to worry about installing an expensive emergency spillway but could handle the water flowing out of the pond with two six-inch overflow pipes through the pond bank. Should the water level rise fast in a really heavy downpour, the pond is so graded that the water would run off on the side where the soil has not been disturbed, not over the bank built up with soil out of the excavation. The water from the spring runs into a control box, where it can be directed by gravity into a pipe leading to the pond or a pipe leading away from the pond. "It took about seven days to fill it at five gallons a minute," says Danny. "Now I'm afraid I spend too much time just staring at it. Water is kind of hypnotic, the way it reflects the trees around and the clouds."

> It is a soothing employment on one of those fine days in the fall when all the warmth of the sun is fully appreciated, to sit on a stump . . . overlooking the pond, and study the dimpling circles which are incessantly inscribed on the otherwise invisible surface amid the reflected skies and trees. (Thoreau, *Walden*)

Danny stocked the pond with bluegills and a little later added bass. "I'll probably put some sterile grass carp in it eventually to keep down waterweeds. I'm just kind of experimenting my way along." The fish are so tame from being fed that they follow Danny around the pond like a flock of sheep. He laid large flat rocks on the pond floor, then propped them up on the downside of the sloping bottom with cement blocks so that there was room underneath for the fish to hide from predators and glaring sunlight.

I asked him why he wanted a pond badly enough to spend sixteen hundred dollars for a liner, since I know how sparing he is with money. For example, he sees no sense at all in buying a new car when an old pickup is cheaper and so much more useful. His first answer surprised me.

"Well, the Metropolitan Sewer District took away our creek and all the fish in it, so I thought we really ought to have *some* natural water around here. What are the wild things supposed to do?" A bit of bitterness creeps into his usual relaxed tone of voice. But he decides not to dwell on a subject that I know is very emotional for him. "I also wanted a place to swim. It is extremely hot working at the forge in summer. Now I can just go jump in the pond and cool off." He pauses again, watching the bees congregate at the pond edge where we are standing. "And as you can see, the pond is really crucial for the bees."

Hundreds of them are winging constantly between the hives and the pond, alighting on pebbles barely sticking above the edge water. A careless bee, or perhaps one newly emerged from the larval stage and not experienced in the ways of life yet, dips too far into the water and buzzes on the surface, unable to fly away. Danny carefully reaches down, puts the palm of his hand under the bee, and lifts it gently into the air until its wings dry enough so that it can fly again. He smiles. It is obvious he gets an enormous pleasure out of the pond. "I've watched a long time, and I'm pretty sure that a bee always returns to the same particular pebble it first landed on."

A lake is the landscape's most beautiful and expressive feature. It is earth's eye; looking into which the beholder measures the depth of his own nature. (Thoreau, *Walden*)

"Actually, I never planned all this out ahead of time," Danny continues, nodding toward the shop, toward his house, back again at the pond. "It just sort of happened, one thing leading to another. Dad's influence was crucial. I don't know about the future. I'd like to get married, but I don't seem to be able to find someone wanting to live like this."

Only a few months after saying that, Danny did find a partner, Stacy Riddle, "wanting to live like this." True to form, instead of buying her an engagement ring, he made one. He bought two ounces of white gold and forged it, not by a jewelry maker's methods but by nineteenth-century techniques, into a ring. He had to make a bit to drill out the mounting for the stone, a beautiful sapphire. Then came the delicate handwork of filing five prongs on the ring to hold the stone in place. "Most rings have four or six prongs. I wanted mine different," he says. The ring is unbelievably fine and delicate for a piece of jewelry made in a home shop specializing in forging steel.

As of this writing, Danny and Stacey have a child. Stacey has decided that she will take up her father-in-law's market gardening (Paul Sr. has, in the meantime, passed away) with a few additions of her own. The spring stream that feeds the pond has always grown a handsome crop of watercress. Because the suburban houses near the creek had septic tanks before the coming of the sewer, most people were afraid the water might be contaminated and the watercress unsafe to eat. (Both Danny and I, as well as several others, have often eaten it with no ill effect, just to prove a point.) But with Stacey on the scene, she and Danny had the water tested. Sure enough, it was safe. No bacteria. She plans to market the gourmet salad plant.

What's the next project Danny has in mind? He smiles. "I think maybe I'll build an outhouse."

ANDREW WYETH'S POND

Monet was not the only artist who was or is a pond lover. The Victorian landscape painters of rural scenes could not resist painting ponds, which stood out like gems reflecting the sky, around which the life of the farm revolved. The paintings unwittingly left a record of how important farm ponds have always been to the economy of rural life, supplying water for livestock, ducks, geese, fish, ice, irrigation, fire protection, and, most of all, water-powered mills. It is not surprising, then, to find that America's foremost living artist, Andrew Wyeth, is also a pond lover. The farm pond he has painted so often belonged to the Karl Kuerner family for three-fourths of a century and is now, along with the farm around it, a national treasure, donated by Karl Kuerner Jr. to the Brandywine Conservancy to preserve it from encroaching suburbia.

The farm is certainly the most famous one in the world. Its house, barn, and landscapes, and the Kuerners who farmed it, serve as models for hundreds of Andrew Wyeth's paintings known throughout the world. When I was younger, writing a book about Andrew Wyeth, I frequented the farm because to me it was like walking through a living art museum of his paintings. I felt as if I were viewing Michelangelo's *David* and the statue spoke to me.

The pond, now being restored at Wyeth's insistence, after years of neglect, is geographically and figuratively the centerpiece of the farm. It lies along Ring Road in Chadds Ford, Pennsylvania, in front of the ancient Kuerner farmhouse. In that house, used as a hospital for American soldiers in the Revolutionary War, Washington and Lafayette laid their plans for running the British out of the Brandywine Valley. As a child Andrew played here with the Kuerner children. His home was just over the hill, and his studio still is. He started painting the farm at about age sixteen, in 1933, and has continued to do so to the present (2002). Recently when I was talking to Karl Kuerner III, a painter in his own right and the third generation of his family on the farm, I mentioned how remarkable it was that Andrew, as well as Karl himself, continues to find inspiration on that little hardscrabble homestead and to render it in paint in a way the whole world honors. Karl nodded and replied, "And Andy remarked recently that 'we haven't hit the tip of this iceberg yet.'"

During the late sixties I was convinced (still am) that fate had allowed me the singular good fortune to cross paths with one of the greatest artists of all time, and I intended to make the most of it if I could. To me, meeting Andrew Wyeth (by chance in a crossroads diner) was like having the chance to know Leonardo da Vinci. So I hung out at the Kuerner farm whenever my work would allow, knowing that Wyeth came there nearly every day to paint. I hoped to learn how he could take the reality of that place and abstract it into what was for me the very essence of reality, especially the reality of farming. Wyeth is not an abstract painter in the classical sense, but the excruciating realism he depicts was to me the ultimate abstraction, the ultimate art. I was convinced that it was possible to do with words what he did with paint, and I was struggling to learn how. I figured, mistakenly of course, that if I hung out at the Kuerners' farm, I would somehow absorb his magic.

I got to know the Kuerner family fairly well, and I still maintain close ties with Karl Jr. and especially the artist of the family, Karl III, and his wife, Louise. Louise keeps her Percheron driving horse on the farm, and the horse is now no doubt as famous as the farm, because Wyeth has used it as the subject of two paintings, *Karlanna* and *Fenced In*. Karl III has painted it dozens of times.

But except for one long conversation and several brief ones, Wyeth avoided me. I did not understand why, since he was a very friendly person, until many years later, when readers of my books started wanting to visit me. I enjoy visitors, but it takes only a few to disrupt painting or writing for days. Hundreds of thousands clamored after Wyeth. He was too polite to say what E. B. White once told a would-be visitor: "Please do not come. There are thousands of you but only one of me."

The pond is the focal point or background detail of many Wyeth paintings. I think immediately of *Brown Swiss* (1957), the painting that first gave me an inkling of the meaning and function of art. There are none of Karl Kuerner's Brown Swiss cattle in *Brown Swiss*, which is just like Wyeth. A viewer familiar with the farm has a feeling that the cows just went into the barn—their beaten paths across the somber meadow above the pond show plainly enough. Wyeth says that he at first put trees and cows into the wide-open expanse on the right side of the painting but eventually took them out to keep from making the scene too trite. He says in his *Autobiography* that he wanted the painting "to be almost like the tawny brown pelt of a Brown Swiss bull."

What one actually sees in the painting only remotely resembles the real scene from which it is abstracted. The painting appears to show a late fall or early winter pasture field—I say "appears" because even with an intimate knowledge of pasture fields, I can't tell for sure what time of year the painting depicts. It is All Time. On the left side is a ghostly, gaunt house; at the far right, some rocks. In the middle a pond glints like a silvery quartz arrowhead. It is a picture not of physical earth, pond, rocks, or house, but of the *soul* of these objects, a spare, stark specter of brown and white that is so unreal that it is real, or perhaps so real that it is unreal. I remember that when I first saw the painting, what riveted my gaze was not any of these soul-objects but a wee bit of fence-soul to the right of the house. The fence is rendered with digitally clear detail and focus, but it does not begin or end in any logical manner. It appears to be just a little stretch of fence DNA, without fence purpose, to me the perfect abstract rendering of both the purposefulness and purposelessness that characterize life.

The canvas is rather large, thirty inches by sixty inches, but the austerity and emptiness of the right side of the painting makes it seem as big as the whole world if you look right into it without reference to anything outside the frame. The pond seems as immense as the ocean, or as Wyeth himself described it, "the lucid pond looking almost like the eye of the earth reflecting everything in creation." The real house sits high enough on the hill behind the pond so that if you stand on the hillside across Ring Road from it, you can see it reflected in the water, as Wyeth paints it—*exactly* as you would see it if you had trained yourself to see as carefully as Wyeth sees and you had eyes as good as a hawk's. In this instance he renders the reality that a camera might record and then a reality that a camera would be unable to portray. Looking at the painting, the viewer can see into the windows of the house, but in the reflection below, the *ceiling* of the room inside the window is also visible because of the angle of reflection. I was awed that an artist would notice and paint such detail.

Of course, to praise the consummate virtuosity of Wyeth's technical ability only makes me an object of ridicule to the modern champions of "abstraction." What has happened to our culture when skill and reverence for accuracy are denigrated in favor of splashes of color that depict only splashes of color? As Henry Pitz says about Andrew Wyeth in *The Brandywine Tradition:* "Most of the critics [today] speak that retarded language, a deprecation of skill, partly because they are bereft of insight into technical matters. It is impossible to imagine a Renaissance, Baroque or Romantic artist apologizing for his virtuosity—he would glory in it and so would all his audience. He would have a deep joy in the exercising of his natural powers. It is impossible to imagine Wyeth's art without this gift."

Karl Kuerner Sr.'s son, Karl Jr., told me how the pond came to be. "When we were kids we had to make our own toys. I remember how we envied the people who lived in the rental house. They were on welfare, and so they had money for toys. Daddy would not have taken welfare even if he were starving, and would not waste money on toys, for sure. So we made our own. One day we dammed the creek up with rocks and made ourselves a little swimming hole. Daddy liked it so much that he built a bigger pond, the one you see now that Andy has painted so many times."

But the stern father, Karl, had to have in mind a utilitarian pond, not just a swimming pool. "The pond's full of fish," he told me proudly on my first visit to the farm. "We always have our own to eat." In the old days (long before the 1960s, when I was hanging around), he also cut ice from the pond. He pointed to an old building not far away. "That used to be the icehouse. Ice would keep in there almost all year. If you didn't mind the work, it was as good as a refrigerator."

The pond was fed partially by runoff water, but springs kept it full year-round. Almost always, water spilled out the overflow that so often caught Wyeth's eye and then his paintbrush. In *Dam Breast* (1970) he meticulously painted the overflow as a frozen casement of ice with a little water oozing down under it. Only someone who has very closely watched a frozen waterfall begin to thaw can appreciate the full beauty and skill of this painting. In *Evening at Kuerners* (1970) he painted the overflow again as the setting sun made it glitter in the dusky twilight, along with the creek below it. He did this picture when old Karl was very sick, he says in his *Autobiography*. While he was painting, he saw Helga Testorf for the first time. She was caring for the sick Karl. Soon afterward, she would model for his famous Helga series of paintings.

Perhaps that is why in *Overflow* (1978), one of the most renowned of the Helga paintings, the overflow of the pond can be seen through the window behind the reclining nude. Perhaps the sensuous flow of water from the pond somehow reminded Wyeth of the sensuous flow of flesh that he was so painstakingly rendering on canvas.

The pond at the Kuerners' can be seen rather well in two paintings, both called *Easter Sunday* (1975), one of Helga (clothed) and the other of Anna Kuerner. One stands and the other sits on the front porch of the Kuerner house on a snowy day, looking down on the frozen pond. In the painting of Anna, an iron pot hangs from the porch ceiling. In the one of Helga, there is no pot. The pond also appears in the distance, fuzzily, in *Rack at Kuerners* (1983), a picture of deer antlers hanging in the pine tree at the very tip of the hill across the road from the pond. Karl planted the cluster of Austrian pines on the hilltop as shade for his cows, from seedlings he brought over from Germany, so the family tells me. The pines and the hilltop appear in even more paintings than the pond.

The pond also appears in the foreground of the painting *Bull Run* (1976), of cattle running down the Kuerner lane. But in this case the pond is only suggested, not detailed. If you have not stood where Wyeth did when painting the scene, you would hardly know you were looking at the inside of the pond dam. It is the cattle that are important to the painting. Every time I glance anew at it, I think, for a brief second, that the animals are actually in motion.

Only a corner of the pond appears in the haunting *Wolf Moon* (1975), which is one of my favorite paintings, partly because of the story Wyeth tells about it. He got the idea for the painting in the middle of a moonlit night, he says, standing above and behind the house. As he stood there, he could hear Anna, then in her seventies, chopping wood into kindling for her morning breakfast fire. Karl Jr.

told me in 1992 that his mother, then ninety-one, was still rising in the night to chop kindling, all the while carrying on a conversation in German with her cat. (She died just shy of one hundred, still sweeping doorways and tending fires.) Added Karl Jr.'s sister, Louise, with a mischievous giggle: "When I was little, Mother used to start fires with sketches that Andy left on the floor." She paused, relishing the knowledge of how valuable those sketches might have been today. "Andy often played with us when we were children. Later he was always wandering around here, busy at painting something. We all really liked him. I thought he was handsome. But my father was very strict about us not bothering him, and anyway we had too much work to do to bother anyone."

The pond is not the only part of the farm that is spring fed. Water from a spring that rises on the hillside across the road has run by pipe to the house and barn for more than a century. Because the spring is higher than even the top floor of the house, the water runs through the whole house and then the barn by gravity. The water system is a marvel. It requires no pumps and no chemical treatment, and will go on forever so long as humans do not bulldoze or pollute the wellsprings. The water comes out of the ground warm enough so that it does not freeze as long as it stays in motion throughout the system. A perpetual motion machine. The painting that honors this marvel of natural technology is *Spring Fed,* a picture of the water trough inside the Kuerner barn with water flowing in and flowing out again, the trough always full, for over a century. Louise Kuerner told me that this is her favorite painting, mostly because when she was young and working at home, before the pond was built, they would all jump into the water trough to cool off and wash away the itching chaff during haymaking.

Springwater also runs through the springhouse, below the pond. In earlier days, the Kuerners kept their milk and cider cool there. "Sometimes a frog from the pond would get into the springhouse and jump into the large pans of milk cooling in the water," Louise said, her eyes snapping with humor.

"Worse than that," Karl Jr. interjected. "Once when Daddy was about to dump a can of milk at the cream station, he noticed a frog swimming in it. He grabbed the frog real quick and stuck it inside his shirt and just went on pouring like nothing had happened."

Karl and Anna had met as shepherds on a mountainside in Germany. The first World War ended that happy way of life. Karl, out of the German army, where, he told me, he had once been chained to his machine gun and had to kill charging American soldiers or die himself, came to America.

"He often told about how they tied three hand grenades together and threw them under tanks," his granddaughter Cathy recalled in 1992. "Grandfather said that once one of these homemade bombs blew off one tread of a tank only, and the tank turned round and round until it ran out of gas while soldiers from both sides stood by and laughed."

When Karl had made enough money, he sent for Anna and little Louise. Anna never really got over being homesick, her children say, and during the rest of her life suffered periodic bouts of depression, only to rouse herself and go on, taking care of the farm and her family. The night I left the Kuerner farm on my last visit, I saw a touching sight. Louise had mentioned that she had not brought a sweater and was chilly. Anna, age ninety-one, silently and solicitously slipped her own sweater over Louise, who was by this time a grandmother too, with all the devotion and care of a young mother dressing her child.

Life on the Kuerner farm was hard, but the Kuerners made the best of it. "Daddy didn't know much about farming, but he was very good at making cider and whiskey," Karl Jr. recalled. "Desperate for money, he became a moonshiner. He made it on the stove. It was good stuff, they said, and he had a thriving little business for a while."

Anna lived in fear of the moonshine, and when Karl did not come home one evening from delivering milk (and whiskey on the sly), she was terrified. "We had no phone, no way to find out what had happened," Louise recalled. "Daddy had the milk cans, and we didn't have enough of them left to hold the evening and morning milk, so we put it in a big washtub." Again they all laughed at the recollection, even though at the time the situation was far from funny. Karl spent only one night in jail, probably paying off the sheriff in good whiskey. But that was the end of the moonshine business.

Karl Jr. remembered another incident that was not funny at the time but made them all laugh anyway. "Daddy found a big metal silo free for the taking and had it hauled to the farm," said Karl Jr. "We stood it up and filled it with three hundred tons of silage. We were pretty proud of that, but a few days later it fell over. Daddy looked out the window during breakfast and couldn't see the silo against the sky. He turned around to us, mystified, and said, 'Someone stole the silo.' It just seemed so funny we all burst out laughing. And then we fed the silage out with the silo on its side. No problem."

"Daddy wasted nothing," he continued. "He took nails out of an old shed and used them to build an outhouse. When he finally switched from hand-milking to the milking machine, he rigged up a way to use the tractor's manifold as a vacuum pump rather than buy one."

"As soon as I left home, Daddy sold the horses and got a tractor," Louise said dryly, and again all of them laughed.

The Kuerner pond reflects not just an old farmhouse on its placid surface. The house is part of an amazing saga of American history. While Washington and Lafayette planned the battle of the Brandywine downstairs, wounded American soldiers lay screaming upstairs, where, two hundred years later, Andrew Wyeth painted the stern visage of Karl Kuerner under the menacing meat hooks, and the soft, sensuous flesh of Helga Testorf.

The whole of American agriculture could be contained in a history of the Kuerner farm. Sometimes I think that Wyeth is painting that history without knowing it—he says he has no interest in farming as such. Karl Kuerner's experience stretched over centuries. He remembered in Germany cutting grain with a scythe ("You need a little piss on your whetstone to get a scythe really sharp," he once told me). By the end of his life he had traversed from those ancient ways to driving the most advanced tractors of the 1970s. In between, under the most grueling, ruthless, impossible circumstances, he went from being nearly penniless to owning a farm. He farmed with horses long after most farmers had switched to tractors (see Wyeth's painting *Spring Landscape at Kuerners* [1933], which shows Karl's hired man plowing with horses). But when the money became available, he unhesitatingly bought tractors. He used money he made from selling *Spring Landscape at Kuerners,* which Wyeth had given to him. ("Andy was very upset by that," Karl Jr. said, "but that's the way Daddy was.")

I have no doubt that if the Kuerner farm had been farther west, farther from urban sprawl, the Kuerners would have gone on to become big commercial farmers. But their land was surrounded by suburbs fifty years earlier than were farms in the Corn Belt, and the Kuerners had little choice but to sell some of the farm because of rising taxes. As the houses pressed in on them, the Kuerners turned away from commercial farming because of lack of land for expansion. With the resourcefulness they had always exhibited, they adapted. They used their tractors to mow suburban estates rather than hayfields and got paid for doing so. Then they turned around and sold the grass from the estates to developers for mulch or to suburbanites to feed their horses. Then, in the absolute perfection of resourcefulness, they convinced estate owners to allow them to grow corn on the estate land in lieu of having to pay for mowing. The Kuerners fed the corn to their livestock, or sold it to the suburbanites so they could feed it to the wild deer. The Kuerners then hunted, butchered, and ate the deer. If only they had gone one step farther and made sausage and jerky from the venison, as my neighbors do here in Ohio, and sold that back to the suburbanites too, they would have invented the first kind of farming that was truly profitable.

Meanwhile, this farm, with its steadfast roots in traditional farming methods, attracted the painters of the famous Chadds Ford school of art nearby. That meant that at least N. C. Wyeth, Frank Schoonover, Harvey Dunn, and Violet Oakley knew something about real-life farming, and it shows in their work. Because N. C. Wyeth stayed on (and painted on the farm too), his son Andrew, his daughter Carolyn, and Jamie Wyeth, his grandson, all famous painters, became familiar with the farm. So did the painter Peter Hurd (he told me once that he gave Karl a painting for boarding his horse), who married Andrew's sister Henriette, another painter. And now as the wheel of history turns completely around, Karl Kuerner III becomes an important painter of the farm too. What more delicious an example could an art historian find of the notion that art and agriculture are two facets of the same human desire to create something beautiful?

Karl Jr. says that one reason the painters came to the farm was that his father was kind and hospitable to them. "Lots of people around here were suspicious of what they thought were weird characters tramping around on their farms with paintbrushes. But Daddy said that in Germany when he was young, people were accustomed to that sort of thing. He kind of liked the idea. He knew Andy was special. He even gave Andy a key to the house so he could come and go as he pleased."

I asked Karl Jr. why he thought Andy kept coming to the farm to paint. I expected some penetrating observation. His eyes twinkled. "Well, when Daddy was alive, I think Andy kept coming for the cider. Daddy made wonderful cider."

It also seems that N. C. Wyeth discovered a new and practical use for farm ponds, according to an anecdote that Henry Pitz relates in *The Brandywine Tradition*. Once while Wyeth was painting in a field, a bull attacked. How did the painter escape? He jumped into a pond nearby.

THE HOUSE OF SEVEN PONDS

Those who become pond lovers learn to expect the unpredictable from nature, but a wild turkey roosting on the roof of the house? Ken and Dixie Gottfried still shake their heads in wonder. First of all, wild turkeys are only now returning to north central Ohio after a century of absence. Second, they are supposed to be very shy of humans. But this old tom decided in the winter of 1998–99 that he liked the Gottfried home just fine. When he wasn't raiding their bird feeders, he enjoyed a view of the surrounding farm country from the roof of their charming log chalet or from the cottonwood tree next to the house.

The Gottfrieds probably should not be surprised. Knowing how a pond lures wildlife, what can you expect when you build *seven* of them around your house? The Gottfrieds have been farmers all their lives. In "retirement" they built a new house and embarked on a plan of aquacultural landscaping that will simply take a pond lover's breath away. Not only do seven ponds grace the grounds around their house, but a small river flows at one end of their property and a tiny stream runs below the house. The lawns around the ponds are impeccably landscaped with flowers, trees, shrubs, and retaining walls of giant blocks of sandstone from an ancient, abandoned bridge. Through the three-story expanse of windows on the great room of the house, the Gottfrieds can watch what goes on in their natural paradise from almost any part of the house.

And watch they do. In fact, if they did not keep close watch, wildlife might not only "grace" their home but take it over completely. Great blue herons, considered rather uncommon in this Ohio farmland, practically flock to the ponds to prey upon the fish. The Gottfrieds recently installed carved blue-heron decoys in all the ponds in the hope of discouraging real ones from approaching. (They can't say yet whether this ploy works.) The smaller water-lily ponds can be covered with protective screening, the only proven way to deter diving and wading birds. An inconspicuous electric fence keeps the couple's mute swans on their designated pond and out of the water lily ponds. A large flock of Canada geese, a species rapidly becoming an outright pest in the East and Midwest, seems deterred too, although they could fly over the inconspicuous fence. A few wild mallards have also adopted the Gottfrieds and waddle around as if they own the place. They might multiply and become a nuisance were it not for foxes, say the Gottfrieds. The mallard hens will not flee the nests they establish along the creek during the hatching season and so become easy prey.

Raccoons almost make bird feeding impossible, since they seem to be able to master the most ingenious feeders designed to prevent them from eating the birdseed. The Gottfrieds keep a live trap set on the patio; otherwise the masked raiders would overrun them.

Deer, though commonly seen along the river, where the Gottfrieds have fostered a wide strip of trees and groundcover for more than a mile along the banks, have not yet begun to eat the ornamentals, since they have plenty of corn, soybeans, and tree brush to nibble in the lush surrounding farmland. The flock of mute swans stays on the pond closest to the house, where there is no electric fence. During mating season, the male, named Ivan the Terrible, becomes quite territorial. "I'd like to have a video of him chasing me when I'm mowing around the pond," says Ken. "Quite comical."

Most of the ponds are laid out so that water will flow from one to the other by gravity. The water level is controlled ingeniously by standpipes. Four of the ponds, the large swan pond and the three small lily ponds, are positioned on descending levels, so that the water from the swan pond moves by gravity through a hidden sand filter bed and down a little waterfall into the second pond. When that pond rises to the proper level, the water flows out another standpipe and through underground pipe into the next pond, and so on. Water to the upper (swan) pond is pumped from a collection basin along the creek. The creek is fed by springs and a field-tile drainage system.

The fifth and largest pond draws water from Brokensword Creek, the small river nearby, through an inlet pipe that is graded backward from river to pond so that water flows by gravity into a collection basin at the pond. It is then pumped into the pond when necessary. This pond is most like a typical farm pond, being about two acres in size and six to eight feet deep, full of game fish like bass and bluegill. A floating aerator keeps the oxygen content high enough and the water stirred enough to avoid fish kills from oxygen depletion. Water from this pond flows by gravity and standpipe to a sixth pond, a small, shallow one devoted to water lilies and other unusual water plants, and stocked with koi, the exotic kind of carp now so popular. Koi are quite colorful, white or black or brilliant shades of yellow, orange, and red with black speckles. They eat algae, keeping the pond water relatively clear. Surprisingly, the Gottfrieds do not stock white amur or grass carp in their ponds to eat waterweeds. Ken says he's been told that they eat minnows too, possibly a plus in most farm ponds but not in a pond full of expensive koi. The Gottfrieds feed the koi standard fish food as a supplement. As Ken throws the pellets into the water, the fish come lazily to the surface and feed. Matching the colors of the fish and the colors of the water lilies, the steep bank on one side of the pond is covered with ranks of low-growing juniper and rows of bright red salvia. In the water float wondrously attractive "islands" of impatiens.

The construction of these floating flower barges is ingenious, similar to that used at Disneyland. The base is made from two pieces of Styrofoam, each two inches thick and four feet in diameter. A piece of felting material is placed over the Styrofoam to help hold water, and over the felt about four inches of potting soil is piled. A little wire fence goes around the outside diameter of the floating flower bed to hold the potting soil in place. Down the middle of the bed is a hole into which a wick of felting material runs into the pond to bring water up to the soil. The impatiens plants are set into the soil, and they rapidly spread to cover the whole bed, the blooms forming a dome shape naturally. With the right amount of soil and no more, the beds will float at just about the right level in the water to suit the plants. Impatiens are supposed to like shade, but these grow "like crazy" in full sun. The floating beds have to be anchored with tie lines to the middle of the pond or they will float to the banks.

The impatiens—indeed all the plantings in the landscape—grow with great health and vigor. To achieve that, along with skillful use of water, the Gottfrieds make their own soil, one part poultry manure and two parts leaf mulch with a little sand mixed in for greater porosity.

The seventh pond, a shallow one, the first that Ken built when he was experimenting with design, receives water from the river and at present is overgrown with algae. There is about a foot of dirt on top of the plastic liner that covers the bottom of the pond. The Gottfrieds plan to turn it into a lotus pond. The hardy lotus is usually *not* a water plant to introduce to your pond, because in short order it will simply take it over completely. (It will grow to the surface from as much as eight feet deep, and there is hardly any way to kill it except with herbicides.) But the Gottfrieds want the lotus to take over this pond so that its huge blossoms will, in summer, turn it into a rampantly gorgeous display of pink color and sweet perfume.

Maintaining such a large, complex, and beauteous landscape is not easy, of course, and Ken likes to describe his efforts humorously as the sixty-forty method. "Forty percent of what we did originally turned out to be a mistake and had to be done over or needed some adjustment," he explains.

For example, herons, both the little green and the great blue, like to land on the floating beds. To discourage them, Ken stuck upright, dowellike sticks unobtrusively among the flowers.

The barely visible electric fence, with small fiberglass posts, was another "adjustment" that has turned out to be most appropriate. The fine wire is merely taped to the self-insulating posts. Posts and wire are easy and cheap to erect, and the fence is hardly noticeable. But it keeps the swans away from rare water lilies, which they might eat. The swans won't fly over the wire because their wings are clipped, a necessity anyway to keep them from flying away. As Ken puts it with his wry humor, "Watching a three-hundred-dollar bird fly away into the wild blue yonder is not a consoling sight."

As part of the landscape design, the Gottfrieds surrounded the bases of trees with flowers of various kinds, but they soon learned that the tree roots grab all the moisture in dry weather and leave the flowers withering. So Ken ran one-inch plastic pipe underground to these flower beds and installed soaker hose under the flowers to keep them thriving. He learned that the pipes did not have to be drained in winter if all valves were left open so that no water pressure could build up in the lines.

One "rule" of pond construction the Gottfrieds ignored rather deliberately. The soil along the Brokensword tends to be generally gravelly or sandy, and they were warned that ponds on this soil wouldn't hold water. The Gottfrieds understood that but also knew that springs were plentiful, not to mention the river and the creek, which receives water from the underground tile draining the large fields above the homesite. Their farm has traditionally been called Indian Springs Farm, in fact, and they felt that they could maintain proper water levels in the two bigger ponds (from which water flows to the smaller ponds). This turned out to be more or less true: the first year the ponds didn't hold water very well, but Ken could supply the water needed from river and creek. By the second year the ponds started sealing themselves as tree leaves fell into them and rotted on the pond floors. There was also an accumulation of a kind of "blue mush," as Ken describes the very fine clay that is also present in the soil, which helped seal the ponds. Normally, Ken points out, leaves are undesirable in ponds, because in rotting they rob oxygen from the water and may cause fish kills. That's one reason why he installed aerators in both of the bigger ponds. The aerators also move some of the bottom water constantly toward the top. This helps alleviate the problem of water inversion, when bottom water suddenly rises or turns over to the top. Water inversion is a common cause of temporary oxygen loss and fish kills in artificial ponds. The rippling effect of the aerators also floats algae to the pond edges, where Ken can treat them easily by walking on the bank and dabbing blue vitriol (copper sulfate) in an old sock or similar cloth material on the algae.

To hold water, the smaller water-lily ponds all have heavy liners of Visqueen, a kind of plastic film that is especially treated so that sunlight will not cause deterioration. One site chosen for a pond was also the location of a spring. That might seem an advantage at first glance, but in this case, not so. The springwater would have continued to ooze up around and outside the pool walls. Ken figured that with a pool liner separating the springwater from the water in the pool, the latter would act as a weight to keep the natural water underground. He learned that springwater has powerful force. It pushed the liner up. He had to go back into the area with drain tile, drain the spring away to the river, and then reinstall the pond and liner. To hide pond liners, he used attractive sandstone blocks as supporting pond walls. They came from an abandoned railroad bridge, free except for the cost of moving them with heavy equipment.

Another "sixty-forty" adjustment will come eventually, because, as Ken points out, he planted the ornamentals too close together, and now bushes hide much of the beauty of various sandstone retaining walls. "If you plant ornamentals so that they are spaced just right when young, they become too crowded later on," he says. "If you space them far apart in anticipation of future growth, they seem too sparse in the early years." He chose to plant them too close together so that they looked right when small and plans to thin the plantings when they start to overgrow the walls.

Behind every decorative use of landscape there is a practical purpose. Flowers are arranged and positioned so that at all times in the growing season, there will be an explosion of blooms. Lots of yellow irises decorate the creek banks but also serve to hold the banks against erosion. "Islands" of black-eyed Susans in the lawns hide old stumps. Wisteria climbs a dead elm. Bittersweet climbs live trees, aided by plastic mesh left over from a peacock pen, wrapped round the tree trunks. (Dogs got into the pen and killed the peacocks.) The Gottfrieds like to use juniper liberally in their landscaping, including rarer strains like Calgary and blue rug, but here again there is a practical as well as decorative purpose. These very low growing junipers hold soil along erosive banks.

Even the "totem pole" rising high over the largest pond is not just for decor. It's an electric pole. Ken had a chain saw artist carve and paint Native American motifs on the pole in the spirit of the farm's name, Indian Springs.

Considering the Gottfrieds' penchant for combining practicality with beauty, it comes as no surprise that Ken has also built a greenhouse next to the Brokensword, in the shadow of his grain-drying and storage bins, for growing his own hydroponic vegetables and for rooting landscaping plants from cuttings. He roots the cuttings on benches inside plastic film cages, with rooting powder applied to the tips of the cuttings. But he also learned that a little twig of willow tied to the cutting encourages it to root.

But more than that, this greenhouse for a time produced a rather unusual crop of fish, especially koi. Koi cost "only" a couple of dollars each as minnows but can grow to be worth a hundred dollars each, or as much as ten thousand dollars for very rare colorations. Ken started minnows in one of several tanks running the length of the greenhouse, and as they grew, he moved them to larger tanks in succession. From there he transferred them to outside tanks for grow-out and/or transfer to the ponds around the house. The outdoor tanks are each about fifteen feet in diameter. Depth can be regulated by standpipe to a maximum of about three and a half feet.

He started the fish in the greenhouse in late winter, getting a free ride on the heat needed for the plants. When warm weather arrived in earnest, the fish could be "set out" in the outside tanks, just as the plants could be set out in the gardens.

"You would never guess what the flaw was in this plan," Ken says with a smile. "It was another sixty-forty situation. I could raise the fish fine. But in the outdoor tanks, the kingfishers came in here in numbers that I could hardly believe. They would sit up on the light pole over the tanks and dive for fish. Left to their own devices, they would have cleaned me out. But that wasn't the half of it. I found that they dove clear to the bottom of the tanks and slashed holes in the liner with their beaks!" The solution was to cover the tanks with suitable strong screening, a troublesome and expensive alternative.

Ken had originally toyed with the idea of going into commercial koi production if his experiment worked out. He even had his own soybeans and corn to use for feed. He shrugs now. "There's a lot of detailed handwork and know-how involved. I decided that this far north I couldn't compete commercially with the Japanese or the

Florida growers." Now he uses the outside tanks to grow potted water lilies and other water plants started in the greenhouse.

Such is life at the House of Seven Ponds, if not Seven Gables. The Gottfrieds greet each day with keen expectancy. They wonder what form of wildlife will appear next or perhaps literally knock on their door. So far no alligators have shown up, they say facetiously. And then someone in the family is bound to repeat: So far.

AN AMISH BISHOP'S
SWIMMIN' HOLE

The greatest strength and at the same time severest weakness of the human brain is its power of abstraction. Humans want to categorize and classify everything under the sun, the better to surround mentally everything that exists and therefore, we hope, understand the infinitude of the universe. The scientist wants to be able to say, often pompously, that such and such a tree is, for instance, a shagbark hickory, *Carya ovata:* the use of the scientific name allows him to converse with other scientists the world over and know they are all speaking of the same tree. But artful hickory-nut hunters, be they humans or squirrels, know so much more about *Carya ovata,* though they have never heard of the Latin label. Hickory-nut lovers know there is an almost infinite variation within the species. The nuts vary by size, shape, taste, shell thickness, shell color, resistance to disease and worms, tightness of husk, maturity time, and productivity. The woodworker knows that the wood of some shagbarks, but not others, looks like pecan and is sometimes sold as such. My sisters, inveterate hickory-nut lovers, have the shagbarks in their woods named, and not with Latin abstractions, either: Big White, Long John, Almond,

Easy Cracker, Bullnut, and so on. Who knows the most, the scientists or my squirrelly sisters?

In the same way, if I write the words *Amish farmer,* human brains will immediately picture to themselves, each according to its own knowledge, an abstract image of what the phrase means to them. Since the image is of no particular Amish person, the knowledge is rather meaningless, but handy. If I use the word *author,* human minds once more evoke an image that they think represents authorship, but, not being of any particular author, the abstraction is again mostly useless knowledge. If I use the word *naturalist,* the brain will likewise conjure in its mind's eye a notion of a naturalist, abstracted from all the naturalists (if any) known to that particular mind. Not only is the knowledge useless, but, as in the other two examples, it could be quite erroneous.

The weakness of this kind of knowledge is not only its lack of particularity but its tendency to make its classifications mutually exclusive. Thus relying only on abstraction, the mind is apt to conclude that an Amish farmer could not be a naturalist in the scientific sense of the term, let alone an author.

What then can I say about David Kline, who is an Amish farmer, a published author, and a respected naturalist? And that's only the beginning of the way he defies classification. He may be the only Amish bishop who loves baseball (in our younger years I got two strikes on him once, before he smacked another line drive past my ear) and who still loves to fish and swim in his own farm pond. Not even Linnaeus could have found a Latin name for him.

David enjoys his farm more than any farmer I have met, and that's an army of them. He and his family make a living milking and caring for a herd of Jerseys. But so great is his love of nature that at times when he talks, I get the impression that farming, however in love with it he is, is just an excuse to give him the time and opportunity to watch the myriad forms of wildlife that live on or travel across his farm.

If you ask him how many kinds of waterfowl he has seen on his acre pond, have a tape recorder handy. He reels off the names faster than I can write: mallard, canvasback, red head, buffle head, hooded merganser, black duck, gadwall, northern shoveller, blue-winged teal, green-winged teal, pintail, ring-necked duck, lesser scaup, ruddy duck, wood duck. He takes a breath. In addition to ducks, there's the white-footed goose, snow goose, Canada goose, osprey, common tern, black tern, ring-billed gull, green heron, great blue heron, and kingfisher. The most unusual waterbird he has seen at the pond, he says, is the northern phalarope, which rarely travels so far inland from eastern coastal waters.

"Once a tundra swan, formerly called whistling swan, alighted here with a flock of Canada geese," he recalls. "The tundra is much larger and was therefore easy to spot. We were quite surprised, since this swan rarely stops at farm ponds on its migratory flights. This one was limping, which may explain how it got separated from its own flock. It had a difficult time getting airborne again, but once its powerful wings took over, you'd never know it had a bad leg."

Do so many different birds visit ordinary farm ponds like his everywhere? Probably. Most of us just aren't accomplished enough at birdwatching to recognize them or don't spend the time necessary to spot them. David can see his pond from his front yard and goes out into the pasture next to it frequently, sometimes daily, to bring in the cows for milking or the workhorses for harnessing. His family also spends many hours fishing, swimming, and ice skating on the pond.

The pond measures a little less than an acre in size and is partly an excavated pond and partly an embankment pond. The water for the pond is almost all from a spring farther up the hill, channeled into the pond through a two-inch pipe. True to Amish efficiency, the water first fills a concrete cattle trough on its way downhill and then flows on into the pond. That way, the cattle and horses do not have to tramp the pond bank to get a drink. Also, runoff water from about five acres flows into the pond when it rains. The dam was formed from the dirt dug out for the pond hole. Originally the pond was fourteen feet deep and has probably subsided a little, as ponds do, to ten or twelve feet deep. David had it built in 1971 and scooped and cleaned it out in 1993. The dirt was added to the back side of the dam to strengthen it. The pond sprang a slow seep leak once, even though it has a good clay core in it, but more fill dirt packed over the seeping area on the back side of the dam solved the problem. I also suspect, as is true of many ponds, the settling of mud inside the pond over the years helped seal the leak. The pond has a grassed emergency spillway off to the side on original, undisturbed soil, not over fill dirt. In flood times water can flow through this spillway rather than over the dam, washing it away. There is also a six-inch outlet pipe to carry away normal overflow. The outlet pipe is screened with heavy hardware cloth all around. "When perch can hear trickling water, like the water going down the overflow pipe, they are attracted to it and try to follow it," says David. "Without the screening, they'd go right down the pipe." Mallard ducks, for some strange reason, went down the pipe too, before the screening was installed. "They died, of course, and we had to go in through the outlet end of the pipe to get them out."

There is also a pipe through the bottom of the dam to drain the pond if necessary. It has a brass valve on it. "I have a steel rod I can hook into the valve to open it. Someone has to snorkel down to the valve to hook it in."

Because the pond is fed by springwater, the Klines tried brown trout in their pond, but the fish didn't survive. Then they stocked largemouth bass, bluegills, and perch. "The standard advice is to stock three hundred bluegills to one hundred bass, but we did just the opposite and have liked the results. We put about a hundred perch in, too. We eat the bluegills and the perch, but not many bass. We like bluegills and perch better, and by keeping the bass population high enough to eat many of the yearly hatch of bluegills and perch, the ones that remain grow to a nice large size rather than stay runty like they do in ponds where they overpopulate," says David. "We've taken sixteen-inch perch out of the pond." The Klines not only fish in summer but ice fish in winter too. "We hardly ever eat fish when the water is warmest, in midsummer," says David. "Fish don't taste as good then." To catch perch, they use waxworms. "I don't know how many meals' worth we fish out every year. I suppose fifteen or twenty. Sometimes we freeze the catch so we always have fish to eat on hand."

"Swimming in a pond in ninety-degree weather is pure bliss," David says, quoting from his book about nature on his farm, *Scratching the Woodchuck*. "I like to get into an inner tube and float quietly along the edge of the pond at frog eye level. You can see the most amazing things that way. Once I was watching dragonflies laying eggs on the leaves of grasses sticking out of the water. I pointed my finger up out of the water. Sure enough, a dragonfly settled down and laid an egg on it."

The pond stays clear of weeds and algae, and there is only a sprinkling of duckweed around the edges. The edge water is fairly shallow, too shallow by proper standards, but there are no emergent weeds. "The pond receives absolutely no care from us," says David. "The muskrats do most of the work of keeping weeds under control. The ducks eat some, too. Possibly because the springwater keeps the pond cooler than rainwater ponds, there is less algae."

How about grass carp for weed control? "No, we don't have any in the pond." He smiles. Humor is never far from his conversation. "Do you know how to fix a carp for the table? Gut the fish, stuff it with horse manure, and bake it in a rubber boot. Then throw away the fish and eat the boot."

A marvelously diverse food chain has established itself in the pond. In addition to the fish and the regular visits of waterfowl, the pond is home to six kinds of frogs: leopard frogs, pickerel frogs, green frogs, bullfrogs, and occasionally spring peepers and chorus frogs. Painted turtles and snapping turtles are residents also. "I saw an absolute monster of a snapper this year," says David. "Its feet and claws were as big as my hands, and when it swam away, its head stuck out twelve inches from its shell. Snappers are heavy predators on other pond life. So be it. Seems like everything is in balance."

The food chain in his pond is more complicated than I, or David, can describe. "The great blue herons and the little green herons take their share. The bullfrogs eat fish spawn, and the bass eat tadpoles. Watersnakes eat minnows. The bass will eat snakes. Everything is eating everything else, and that's why we don't get too many little fish in the pond, I guess. I see clouds of tiny minnows in the spring. Something eats most of them."

He saw a huge watersnake in the pond this year. "I was very glad about that. In recent years the watersnakes seem to have become scarce around here. I like to think that because we are farming organically and trying to maintain all kinds of habitat for wildlife on our farm, maybe we are attracting more of nature than would otherwise be the case."

David shifts easily from talking about the pond to talking about the pasture full of cows next to it. It is obvious that to him, pond and pasture are parallel food systems: the fish graze the pond; the cows graze the pasture. The Klines follow a "new" way to farm called grass farming, which is really a very old way slicked up a bit with modern know-how. Ideally in grass farming, cows or other livestock live almost exclusively on what they can graze on pasture, just as the fish live exclusively on the food that the pond provides. The parallel is not exact, because dairy cows need supplemental grain for profitable milk production. But the change of focus from feeding cows a ration based on corn and only a little seasonal pasture, which is the common way, to feeding them on pasture for a longer period of time and less grain in the barn provides significant savings.

I walked with David across the pasture on his daily chore of "moving the wire." The pasture we were in, of about fifteen acres, was divided into three long strips by single electrified fence wires.

Across the width of the strip being grazed was another strand of wire. Every day after the evening milking, David moves this cross wire up a little, so that the cows get a meal of fresh, new grass daily. It takes about twenty days to go through all three strips in this manner, by which time the cows can start over. Remarkably, the pasture will last most of the growing season this way, with an occasional diversion to other temporary and emergency pastures in periods of dry weather. By skillfully rotating these pastures and by using improved grasses and legumes, he and his sons and son-in-law have extended the grazing period to about eight months.

"Some cows take to it better than others," says David. "If we select cows for high performance on grass instead of high performance on corn as farmers have been doing for years, grass farming can only improve in efficiency. And it's very efficient already. We may be at the beginning of a new era in farming, when the animals by grazing take care of the weeding and harvesting, and the need for tractors, fuel, and expensive machinery is as greatly reduced on all farms as it already is on Amish farms."

JANDY'S POND

Jandy's pond was dug, among other reasons, to provide soil for a garden, making literal the observation that gardens and ponds go well together. But the story of Jandy's is something more than that.

Andy Reinhart was giving a speech about how he and his wife, Jan Dawson, who together operate Jandy's, make a living growing vegetables and flowers for direct retail sale on less than two of their forty, mostly wooded, acres. The inevitable question came up, in the usual tone of disbelief: You say you are making your *entire* living from less than two acres? Andy, who, like Jan, is about fifty years of age, cocked his head slightly, staring at nothing in particular, as he habitually does when he is thinking about how to word an answer. He was not really thinking about his answer, which was an easy one, but about how the questioner was going to react.

"Well, yes."

"You're saying you can live on ten thousand dollars a year?"

A hush spread over the audience. Andy paused. "Well, yes," he said again. "The first year I lived here alone, in a little cabin built with recycled material, I kept my expenditures under a thousand dollars while earning a good factory wage."

A murmur passed through the audience. Some of the people were both awed and impressed. But to my surprise, a few showed not just disbelief but distinct hostility. To the gilded age of the 1990s, it was positively un-American to live that poorly. Heavens, if very many people opted to do as Andy Reinhart does, the economy would collapse. They noted Andy's beard and ponytail, his plain clothing, and concluded that he was one of *those* people—you know, living a mean and scruffy life, ignorant of the niceties of civilization. As his friend, I had a hard time not laughing at them.

Andy actually does have a little money. He had prepared himself for homestead farming in the way that all middle-class people did before the loss of common sense occurred in America. He worked hard for a good wage and lived a spartan existence until he had accumulated enough money to buy some land and finance a start-up on sweat equity, not borrowed money. Part of his earnings had gone into company stock, and when its value rose dramatically on paper during the heady days of the nineties, he was embarrassed. It went against his philosophy of life to make that kind of money. "Neither Jan nor I believe it is right to be making money from someone else's work." So he sold their stock, probably the smartest financial decision he ever made, since soon after that the stock market nose-dived. As the old joke goes, he hasn't spent it all yet farming. "There is a grossly obese behemoth . . . that overshadows our lives," he wrote in the *Ohio Ecological Food and Farm Association News* in 1998. "It's the American Economy. . . . Quit feeding the monster. Stop buying all that 'stuff' we don't need, which would at least slow down the amount of polluted waste the behemoth produces."

The way Jan and Andy live, operating their business under the name Jandy's, is not for everyone, but I don't know why not. They demonstrate daily that living frugally but comfortably is not difficult for anyone with discipline, intelligence, and creativity about spending money. Andy has always lived a parsimonious life, and for a while he wondered if he would find anyone willing to share that life with him. Jan, coming off an impossible marriage, found in Andy exactly what she was looking for: a person who shared her mistrust of the rampant materialism that she believes is destroying cultural stability and common sense in our society. "When I first got to know Andy, when he was living here in that little cabin and working at Honda, he lived on macaroni and cheese and peanut butter sandwiches. Every day he would pack his lunch, and it never varied: a peanut butter sandwich, a slice of Swiss cheese, an apple, and a Little Debbie oatmeal cookie."

When they married, she asked for one major change: "I made him promise to build me a house," she says, laughing. "The little cabin was so small I had to go outside to get enough elbow room to whip up a dish of mashed potatoes."

Their house is a marvel of economy without sacrificing comfort. It is small but not noticeably so, because of the large main living/dining room with kitchen, bath, and bedroom adjoining. The house is mostly underground, but with large windows facing the south for plenty of light all year round and some solar heat in winter. They recently added an enclosed porch so the windows are shaded in the summer. The house is always cool in hot weather without air conditioning and warm in winter with a minimum of fuel. Their fuel is their own wood.

Having apprenticed themselves to frugality rather than to the "American Economy," Jan and Andy had only to continue that lifestyle as they set to work as small-scale farmers. Coming from a farming community, Andy had already learned the practical skills of agriculture, which he now applied assiduously to horticulture. ("You have to be very foolish to try to make a living growing corn, soybeans, and wheat today," he says.) Jan brought another skill to their portfolio. She knew not only her garden vegetables, but how to grow and dry flowers and make dried flower arrangements of extraordinary quality and beauty. Dried flowers quickly became one of the staples of their business.

"The real trick is to start slow and avoid going into debt for expensive equipment," says Andy. "The supply industry can talk a great line about how gearing up for high production will mean high income, but unless everything goes perfectly—and when does that happen?—the grower has a difficult time just paying his debts and must put in long and stressful hours to boot. We have learned to stay at the production level where we can handle everything with our own labor rather than automated machinery and hired help. We end up producing less but not working quite as hard as the high rollers. We make enough net income for our lifestyle. We have time to enjoy ourselves."

Observing how they manage makes me conclude once more that enterprises like Jandy's succeed for reasons that can't be taught but must be learned by a properly attuned and willing mind. Jan and Andy remind me of the late Scott and Helen Nearing. They have deeply felt philosophical reasons for living the way they do. That philosophy, not clever growing techniques, is what makes their market garden profitable. Or to put it another way, they developed the clever techniques because they were committed to the philosophy. How often people who think that they want to live like Jan and Andy fail because they believe that success is something that experts and their manuals can teach them. (Many book and magazine publishers catering to this audience make the same mistake.)

Jan and Andy's canny sense of when to spend and when to keep the billfold folded is phenomenal. Almost everything on their farm has seen duty before it arrives there, including the pickup truck. Huge compost piles, the source of their soil's unbelievable fertility, come from leaves their town is only too glad to truck to their farm. Their sugarhouse, the drying barn for the flowers, the greenhouses, the garden toolhouses, the many kinds of trellises and cold frames, the root cellar, the "new" porch on the house, the throw rugs on the floor (braided from old blue jeans) are all largely built of scrounged or recycled materials—wood, masonry, and native stone. Large plastic tanks obtained free are recycled to catch rainwater from the barn roof to use in watering plants. They found low-priced black locust and catalpa logs no one else wanted (most people do not know that the wood is practically impervious to rot) and had them sawn into lumber for raised beds and greenhouse framing. A discarded TV dish they found, turned upside down and sunk into the ground, became a little fishpond. Discarded computer disks dangle on wires to scare away birds. "The dish and disks are appropriate technology," says Andy, with a little smile.

Their passive solar greenhouse, measuring nine by sixteen feet, is a masterwork of scrounging. The in-ground wood is black locust and the framing rot-resistant black walnut from second-grade boards that were cheaper than white oak. "None of the wood was as expensive as masonry would have been," says Jan. They actually had to pay regular price for the polycarbonate plastic panels on the roof. Nevertheless, the whole structure cost them only $647 out of pocket. To help insulate the greenhouse so that no other source of heat than the sun would be needed, Andy dug a pit with the front-end loader of his little tractor, positioning the floor below ground level. The dirt dug from the pit he pushed back against the walls, providing insulation four feet high around the walls on the outside. The greenhouse abuts the south side of the flower-drying barn and so is shielded from cold north winds. Plants can be started in the greenhouse as early as February without supplemental heat, and on the floor of the greenhouse, salad greens grow all winter.

Jandy's grows almost the whole array of vegetables sold at local farm markets, along with the dried flower arrangements and a large crop of gourds for sale as decoration or birdhouses. Onions (bigger than softballs), tomatoes, elephant garlic (the bulbs averaging a pound each), and asparagus are mainstays, along with several kinds of lettuce, which grow so big under plastic houses that one head will hardly fit into a bushel basket. Chinese cabbage, kale, spinach, peas, beans, and potatoes fill out Jan and Andy's market offerings. Formerly they sold mainly at a large farmers' market in Columbus but now they take their produce mostly to their local market in Bellefontaine and to organic groceries. "Selling in Columbus seemed so impersonal, too big," says Andy. "Also, there was too much of a temptation just to make money." He smiles. "You can make too much money going to Columbus."

Jandy's follows strict organic methods to grow its produce but doesn't sell under an organic label. "We became organically certified, but I'm uncomfortable with the certification philosophy involved," Andy explains. "There's a dramatic dichotomy between the legal letter-of-the-law process of certification and the spirit of the law. For example, it is okay to ship organically certified food thousands of miles to get premium prices, even though long-distance shipping is subsidized by highway taxes and involves tremendous amounts of pollution-causing fossil fuel. Then the produce competes with locally grown food. It also undermines the need for every local area to accept its responsibility for taking care of itself in every way possible.

"Certification also allows a grower to farm thousands of acres of organic food if he or she has the money to hire enough people at low wages or to buy enough fuel-wasting high tech machinery," he continues. "These practices may fulfill the letter of the law, but to me they violate the spirit of the law, the spirit of what organic farming is about. When the letter of the law and the spirit of the law clash, I'm afraid the latter suffers in the name of economic greed. Moreover, you can't guarantee organic purity by certification but only by the character of the grower. Once a farmer hangs up his 'certified' sign, his responsibility shifts from the consumer to the certification board, which can't ride herd on everyone every year. Certification also relieves the consumer of the responsibility to verify for himself that the food is actually organic. We don't know exactly what to call our produce, and I guess that's the point. We don't need a label. A label is not dynamic enough."

Careful economy extends into Jan and Andy's private lives, too. They have dropped their health insurance. They have become assiduous students of alternative medicine and, I believe, know more about the negative effects of mainstream medicine than many doctors do. Andy is a strict vegetarian and does not drink alcoholic beverages. Jan follows suit except when she is visiting evil companions like Carol and me. "We investigate almost all the alternative medical theories," says Jan. "Some of it is so far out that friends think we've gone off the deep end. We don't necessarily believe in all that stuff but are open to the possibility that the scientific, medical, chemical, and pharmaceutical companies may not have our best interests at heart. I've been so awed by the fact that our livers can completely re-grow themselves that I wonder if our bodies have more abilities than we give them credit for."

At any rate, their food and drink come from their own gardens. They have built a large underground root cellar for food storage, keep bees for honey to sell and to eat, and boil down gallons of maple syrup for market and home use. True to their inclinations, the sugar-house walls are made almost entirely of recycled windows out of an old building. The syrup boiler came from a discarded barrel stove, the top cut out with a welding torch to accept the sap pans, the pans scavenged from a junkyard.

Building a pond has been a dream of Jandy's for a long time. Like all successful pond builders, Jan and Andy were in no hurry, wanting to watch how runoff water flows over their property in wet years and dry, so as to choose a spot that rain could keep adequately filled but which would not be subject to a large amount of runoff water, necessitating expensive and complicated overflow designs. Another potential problem was finding a spot that would hold water. Land in their vicinity has the unusual characteristic of being inconsistent in type: either clay with good water-holding capacity or sandy gravel.

Sometimes the two occur close together. Clay loam on top can turn into sandy gravel four feet down (ideal for growing vegetables) but can then return to good water-holding clay below the gravel. First Jan and Andy dug a test hole at the place they wanted to site the pond. The test revealed sufficient clay. But when the pond builder began to work with bulldozer and hydrahoe, he hit a pocket of sand and gravel just beyond the test hole. The only recourse was to see if he could dig through it and hit clay again. Fortunately, this turned out to be true, but the pond of necessity ended up deeper (ten feet) than Jandy's had planned (but which they will be happy about in the future, from my experience). Once the builder hit good clay again, he dug a big trench under and around it and, using clay from the all-clay side of the pond, filled the trench side and packed it down to form a water-impermeable clay core where the gravel had been. The final pond measures about thirty by fifty feet. The pond is close enough to house and barn that the roof water can be guttered and tiled into it. Along with runoff from the land directly above, the roof runoff filled the pond over winter.

"I guess you'd have to say that our pond really is literally part of our gardening," Andy says, again with his whimsical little smile. "One of the reasons I wanted to build it was to use the topsoil from the pond site to fill in low spots in the gardens."

Jan and Andy are the only pond lovers I know (except the ones in the next chapter) who do not plan to stock fish for eating. They avoid fish as part of their vegetarian regimen. "We aren't even going to put fish in it, at least not at first," says Jan. "We want to test the old notion that fish will get in a pond on their own because birds will carry fish eggs on their feet from another pond. I'm not convinced of that." Their main reason for the pond is wildlife. "I love the wood ducks that pass through our place every spring," says Jan. "They land on other ponds in the vicinity, where they are hunted and shot. Wood ducks are about the most beautiful birds I've ever seen, and we want to protect them a little. With the pond close, I will be able to watch them out the window. We hope they will make their homes here and brood in the nests designed particularly for wood ducks that we have installed."

"Also we will use the pond for swimming," says Andy, "and as supplemental irrigation water for the gardens in times of drought."

He took a deep breath as if to say more but then lapsed into silence, and I wondered what he almost said. Later, in a letter, he wrote:

> The real reason for the pond is that it is a good place to sit, lose the distractions of everything that comes out of human intellect, and experience nature. The peace and spirituality of that experience is beyond verbal expression. No matter how gifted one is with words, the experience is only diminished by words. Jan says she believes that when we die we will "know" the meaning of it all. I disagreed until I realized her "knowing" was not of the intellect. In the preface of a book on Zen Buddhism that I found, the author says, "this book is *about* Buddhism, but if you want to *know* Buddhism, you must experience it." I quit reading the book until a few years later because I knew he was right. And at that time I wanted to *know,* not "know about."

A WILD FOOD GATHERER'S
GARDEN POOLS

Peggy Dolinger straightens up from pulling grass out of her purple coneflowers and ponders the water trickling down the mound of rocks into her garden pool. "There's no reason for anyone to go hungry," she says. "There's food growing wild everywhere, and medicine too, along country roads, in unfarmed fields, in fence-rows, along railroad tracks, in the woods, in vacant lots, *everywhere*. Including nuts and berries, there are over a hundred food and medicinal plants in a five-mile radius of our home here. I think it's a shame that this knowledge is being lost, and so I'm teaching it again." She smiles. "Four Native Americans are coming to my classes to learn from this little old white woman what their tradition once would have taught them."

Peggy and her husband, Jim, bought their homestead about ten years ago, deliberately picking a very rural part of a rural Ohio county where population hasn't changed for a century. Stable population is the key to a good place to live for people who want to enjoy life rather than money.

The next time an urbanite asks me whatever do we *do* out here in the country, I intend to send them to the Dolingers' to join Peggy's classes, which meet regularly on their farm. They would learn much more than how to identify and use wild plants. Students see firsthand the wonders that a backyard garden pool can provide, the edible and medicinal plants growing around it, and the rare and unusual landscape plantings, like the weeping Alaskan cedar tree (*Chamaecyparis nootkatensis pendula*) and a ramshorn willow (*Salix babylonica crispix*), whose leaves curl around like the horns on a merino ram. Or they can gaze out over the large farm pond by the barn or contemplate the Japanese rock garden next to the small pool, and realize how every country home, however modest, can be transformed into an Eden of natural beauty and peace as attractive as any park that people travel hundreds of harried, fuel-gulping miles to see.

The demonstration and teaching garden is divided into various plots, according to the use of the plants in them or the environmental niche they fill. Peggy stresses to her students that most of the plants in her garden can be found in the wild, and after a few classes that focus on how to identify the ones she grows, she takes them "grazing" in the fields and along the roadsides around the farm. In addition, she grows unusual and useful plants not often found in the wild. Pointedly, her plantings include few of the vegetables found in normal gardens, although their apple trees produce enough fruit for the apple butter boil-down that the Dolingers hold nearly every year.

There's a fragrance garden, with plants like scented geraniums (pelargonium, which smells like chocolate); anise; hyssop *Agastache foeniculum;* several thymes, including *Thymus* x *argenteus, Thymus* x "Doone Valley," and *Thymus* x *citroiodorus aureus;* and *Pogostemon patchouli,* which must be moved indoors in winter. Peggy makes a body lotion from it.

In the medicinal garden grow mostly native wild plants like bee balm, Culver's root (or Culver's physic, *Veronicastrum virginica,* long used as a mild laxative), althea (a mucilage from this marsh mallow was originally used in making marshmallows; hence the name), comfrey, calendula, several coneflowers, and elecampane (*Inula helenium,* still used commonly in commercial medicines). "A mixture of ca-lendula and comfrey is good for healing," says Peggy, "so good, in fact, that you must wash the wound clean or the salve will heal the skin right over the dirt and maybe cause a problem." Jim, who is not generally as excited about medicinal plants as his wife, swears by coneflower tea, especially *Echinacea purpurea*. "It has kept me free of colds for several years. Fellow workers are using it and claim similar results." Adds Peggy, "Actually, I prefer buying these preparations from quality reputable sources now that they are easily available."

The prairie garden contains gray beardstongue (*Penstemon canescens*), compass plant (*Silphium aciniatum*), prairie dock (*Silphium terebinthinaceum*), wild quinine (*Parthenium integrifolium*), once used to treat fevers, and many others. "Originally, there were areas of tall-grass prairie in this part of Ohio, so we are fortunate in being able to find both woodland and prairie plants here," says Peggy. "I found the prairie dock, which is fairly rare here, growing in a vacant lot uptown."

The Japanese rock garden is a selection of large stones of various shapes, grouped on a surface of white gravel. "The shape, size, and position of the stones signify various spiritual values that have been intrinsic to contemplation gardens in Japan for centuries," says Peggy. There are only a few plants around the rock garden, and they are not flowering specimens. "The idea is not to have any colorful plants to distract the meditation that such a garden is supposed to inspire," she explains. "Just being able to relax and be calm in this garden is good food and medicine in a spiritual sense."

The central focus of all the gardens is the garden pool and the plants growing in and around it. At the far end of the pool, divided from it by a graceful arched footbridge that Jim built, is a marsh garden. The pool is dotted with plants in underwater pots, including night- and day-blooming water lilies and cotton grass (*Eriophorum angustifolium*), plus variegated sweetflag (*Acorus calamus variegata*), variegated pennywort (*Hydrocotyle sibthorpioides*), variegated rush (*Scir-*

pus tabernaemontani zebrinus), water canna, water hyacinth, pickerel rush (*Pontederia cordata),* and parrot's feather (*Myriophyllum aquaticum).* Marsh plants include variegated cattail (*Typha latifolia variegata*), dwarf cattail (*Typha minima*), horsetail (*Equisetum hyemale*), several miniature horsetails, marsh marigold (*Caltha palustris,* which seeds itself), moth mullein (*Verbascum blattaria*), and wild monarda (*Monarda fistulosa*). Unusual plants around the pond include ribbon grass (*Phalaris arundinacea*), porcupine grass (*Miscanthus sinensis strictus*), variegated arborvitae (*Thuja* "Wansdyke Silver"), variegated juniper (*Juniperus variegata*), and elephant ears (*Colocasia esculenta*).

In the water swim koi, flashes of white, orange, gold, silver, gray, and black in the sun. The fish follow visitors as they walk along the pond. "Before feeding time they practically jump out of the water begging for food," Jim says.

The couple used to remove the water lilies and other pool plants for the winter and store them in the basement but have learned that at least in recent winters, milder than usual, they survive at the bottom of the pool.

There is also a tiny oriental water garden, highlighted by a model of a bamboo pump through which water flows into the pool from underground pipe and pump. In the water grow several unusual plants: dwarf papyrus (*Cyperus papyrus nanus*), winter lettuce or shellflower (*Pistia stratiories*), taro (*Colocasia esculenta* Jenkensii Uahiabpele Arac.), and some miniature water lilies.

Finally, closer to the house stands what the Dolingers refer to as the "whimsical water pump," their latest addition to the lawn display. The iron pump is a copy of an old hand pump that is made to work but that Jim connected to a hidden electric pump. Visitors can use the tin cup to get a drink, as in the days of yesteryear, or the water can also flow into a miniature water garden in a wooden tub under the spout. In the tub grow lizard's tail (*Saururus cernuus*), silver water clover (*Marsilea vestita hiruta*), and umbrella palm (*Cyperus alternifolius*).

As I enjoy a Scottish shortbread Peggy makes (flour and butter, flavored with fresh rosemary from the garden and orange peel) I ask her how she moved from an interest in edible and medicinal plants to the pool and water plants.

"Oh, you know, it's all so fascinating. First I got interested in variegated varieties of common plants, which I've always been attracted to. I'd go to plant nurseries looking for them and see the garden pools and the seemingly unlimited number of water plants that could be grown in them. I just had to try it. One thing leads to another."

Peggy thinks of projects to enhance their home, and Jim transforms her ideas into reality. In addition to doing some renovating on the old farmhouse they live in, they have built both the smaller garden pool and the large farm pond near the old barn that dominates the homestead. Then they built a garden arbor house, the Japanese rock garden, a tiny oriental garden pool, a bridge over the larger garden pool, a mound of large rocks that cleverly hides the pipe from which water in the pool is pumped back up to the top of the waterfall, an outdoor rock oven, and a small model of a covered bridge over the creek that wanders through the field below the formal part of their landscaping. They have so many projects lined up for the future that they do not contemplate or plan ever to be finished. "Since I drive a truck over the road all night during the week, I really don't want to travel for a vacation," Jim explains. "We make our home our vacation spot." He smiles ruefully. "I've had about all of the outside world I desire anyway. In a general's book about Vietnam, I'm listed as killed in action. Sure glad that generals are often wrong."

To build the larger garden pool, Jim and Peggy scooped out an area of lawn about three feet deep, six feet wide, and maybe fifty feet long in a graceful curve. They covered the floor of the pond with sand and installed a tough rubber liner over it. Then they began hauling stones from the quarry in their pickup truck—more than seventeen tons' worth, all moved by hand "except that great big one" at the base of the rock mound down which water tumbles into the pool. A concealed pump behind the rocks lining the pool moves the water from the pool through a concealed plastic pipe up to a plastic barrel hidden under the mound of waterfall stones. The barrel is three-fourths full of lava rock chunks. As the water rises in the barrel, it is filtered through the lava and then flows out the top to tumble down the granite stones like a miniature mountain stream. The tumbling also aerates the water.

"The lava rock has to be removed from the barrel twice a year for cleaning," says Jim. "Lava is comparatively light, but it was a difficult job fishing the pieces by hand out of the barrel for cleaning. What I did was install the barrel inside the pile of rocks in such a way that I could remove it easily. On the back side of the rock mound, I inserted a piece of roofing metal next to the barrel and then piled the quarry stones against it. To remove the barrel, I only have to lift away a few outer stones and the piece of metal, and tip the barrel out. Then I tumble the lava rocks with water in our old cement mixer for cleaning."

The only idea that the Dolingers have tried that has not so far been a success is the outdoor oven. Actually, it worked well while it lasted. "We baked a pie in it," says Jim. "The oven would stay plenty hot enough for cooking for several hours after we pulled the coals out, but the stones, we learned, wouldn't take the heat because they were quarry stones from underground and still moist all the way through. The heat shattered them. When we rebuild the oven, we'll use dry fieldstones, and that will solve the problem. Or we'll rebuild it out of clay. Some of the subsoil clay in this area is apparently usable that way. They make bricks out of it."

The farm pond measures about a half acre in size, scooped with a track hoe out of what was once a barnyard. The water is about fifteen feet deep at the center. The subsoil is heavy clay and holds water without any sealant. "We dug a well, installed a heavy-duty pump, and pumped water into the pond for twenty-nine days straight, all day and night," says Jim. "I figure about fourteen gallons a minute, so there must be three-fourths of a million gallons in there."

There is no overflow, since only rainfall goes into the pond. Not having to install overflow pipes or an emergency spillway greatly reduced the net cost of the pond. And if the water level recedes because of evaporation during dry weather, more water can be pumped in. Jim keeps a big aerator/circulator operating in the pond, lifting bottom water to the top and spraying it into the air to keep the water cool and clear and discourage waterweeds. He also adds a bit of an aquatic-plant growth control (Aquashade) to the water to discourage weed growth, and so far (for two years now) the water has remained crystal clear.

Since he and Peggy are allergic to fish and so cannot eat them, he has not stocked any in the pond. Its main use is for swimming. The bottom at the shallow end is covered with many tons of gravel to keep the water from muddying. At the deep end the couple built a raised deck that extends out over the water. "I like to sit here and look at the water," says Peggy. "Makes me feel very peaceful."

HILLSIDE CATCHMENT PONDS

Monet may have finally captured the essence of pond water in paint, but I doubt that pigment could portray the essence of human love for ponds as touchingly as Robert Frost did with these lines from "The Pasture":

> I'm going out to clean the pasture spring
> I'll only stop to rake the leaves away
> (And wait to watch the water clear, I may)
> I shan't be gone long—You come too.

These lines led me, as a child, into a love of poetry. I had always thought that the last three words, "You come too," had been addressed to all readers, in one of those happy strokes of genius. Written any other way, the invitation would seem patronizing, even a bit grandiose (if one can be a bit grandiose). But according to his biographers Frost was addressing not readers in general, but specifically his wife, possibly as a way to make up for a little quarrel or maybe just to lure her away from the house for a moment of quiet companionship. Or maybe more. Learning the personal detail, I have loved the poem as an adult, too. How often do we farmers come to the kitchen door and, under one excuse or another, try to entice our spouses away for a little walk in the fields? Or maybe more.

But pasture springs, dug out of a hillside seep to form little pools for the livestock to drink from, do need to be cleaned out regularly. Even if tree leaves and other debris do not choke the whole surface, they will rot and render the water less palatable. As all husbandry knows, the cleaner the water that livestock have available, the more they will drink and the better they will thrive. Uncleaned, the pool will eventually clog and diminish to a tiny rivulet too shallow for cattle and sheep to drink from and will soak back into the earth a short distance from the point of origin.

Louis Bromfield, the famed novelist and farmer, gave cleaning out little catchment pools a sort of notoriety. (He was an eloquent champion of farm ponds in general, devoting a whole chapter to them in his book *Malabar Farm*.) In my favorite story about Bromfield, he was holding agricultural scientists in thrall in Iowa as he told how the rejuvenation of the soils at Malabar Farm had caused the hillside springs to flow again. Although restoring land to the point where old springs will renew themselves generally takes many more years than Bromfield could have devoted to the task in his lifetime, the learned audience applauded with great exuberance. Bromfield's long-suffering farm manager, Max Drake, was hiding his head in embarrassment. Later Drake would say in humor (and is so quoted in *Return to Pleasant Valley*, edited by George DeVault):

He [Bromfield] had them eating out of his hand. . . . [N]ot only were banks going down that river [because of erosion], the outhouses were going down, the farms were going down . . . he laid it on. "Now . . . that we started to do contour farming, the soil has responded. We've got springs that have started flowing that never flowed for years." Well, we cleaned 'em out, that's the reason they flowed. He didn't say that. He said it was because of contour farming. . . . I got off in the corner and was kind of enjoying what was going on and somebody put their arm over my shoulder . . . [and said], "Max, don't worry about it. Somebody's got to scare the bejesus out of 'em." I never worried about it again. I don't care how much he exaggerated, he got his points across. He got people concerned and just was great. I loved the guy.

A more profound and accurate view of hillside catchment pools comes from Wendell Berry, the Kentucky writer and farmer. In his essay "A Native Hill," in *The Long-Legged House*—the book that so affected me that soon after reading it I changed my life, left the East Coast (as he had done), and went home to the Midwest—he writes:

> Not far from the beginning of the woods, and set deep in the earth in the bottom of a hollow, is a rock-walled pool not a lot bigger than a bathtub. The wall stands nearly as straight and tight as when it was built. It makes a neatly-turned, narrow horseshoe, the open end downstream. This is a historical ruin, dug here either to catch and hold the water of the little branch, or to collect the water of a spring whose vein broke to the surface here—it is probably no longer possible to know which. The pool is filled with earth now, and grass grows in it. And the branch bends around it, cut down to the bare rock, a torrent after heavy rain, other times bone dry. All that is certain is that when the pool was dug and walled there was deep topsoil on the hill to gather and hold the water. And this high up, at least, the bottom of the hollow, instead of the present raw notch of the stream bed, wore the same mantle of soil as the slopes and the stream was a steady seep or trickle, running most or all of the year. This tiny pool no doubt once furnished water for a considerable number of stock through the hot summers. And now it is only a lost souvenir, archaic and useless, except for the bitter intelligence there is in it. It is one of the monuments to what is lost.

Berry is writing here about a walk he was taking over the land of which his farm is a part, hilly land of the lower watershed of the Kentucky River, where he lives and farms and writes. This land has known the footprints and work of his family, among others, back to the days of his great-great-grandparents. As he walks, he is lamenting the ruination of steep land that should never have been broken to the plow. Just a few pages ahead of his description of the pool, he writes:

> It is not possible to know what was the shape of the land here in this hollow when it was first cleared. Too much of it is gone, loosened by the plows and washed away by the rain. I am walking the route of the departure of the virgin soil of the hill. I am not looking at the same land the firstcomers saw. The original surface of the hill is as extinct as the passenger pigeon. The pristine America that the first white man saw is a lost continent, sunk like Atlantis in the sea. The thought of what was here once and is gone forever will not leave me as long as I live. It is as though I walk knee-deep in its absence.

Wendell Berry and his wife, Tanya, returned to this land in 1965 (from New York City, where he had been teaching), and they have spent the time since then trying to heal the farming errors of the past on their farm. He has transformed the "native hill" that he lamented in 1969 into a green jewel of grass upon which, almost any day except in the very dead of winter, livestock and workhorses graze. That hill, deemed marginal land, is now capable of producing almost as much meat, dairy products, and horsepower per acre as rich Corn Belt soil—maybe more than Corn Belt land devoted to industrial corn and soybeans. His hills and his bottomlands are lush with pasture; his woodlands grow decent young timber once more. Only in his desire to bring back the hillside pond, the "monument to what has been lost," has he not succeeded. "I've built four of them, but not one holds water year round," he tells me sadly.

That Berry would want to build ponds at all is somewhat remarkable, because he already spends almost as much time watching water as a seafaring fisherman. His pasture pond is the Kentucky River, beside which he lives. His writing is saturated with the river's water. He ponders it in the same way that all of us landlocked water watchers ponder our ponds. In *The Long-Legged House* he writes: "The river is the ruling presence of this place. Here one is always under its influence. The mind, no matter how it concentrates on other things, is never quite free of it, is always tempted and tugged at by the nearness of the water and the clear space over it." Watching the river in flood, he is awed by its power. "Or, more exactly, an impression of the *voluminousness* of its power," he writes in the same book. "The sense of the volume alone has come to me when, swimming in the summertime, I have submerged mouth and nose so that the plane of the water spreads away from the lower eyelid; the awareness of its bigness that comes then is almost intolerable."

A love of water, specifically of a farm pond, shows up in the work of another writer, Bobbie Ann Mason, author of the acclaimed *In Country,* about the effects of the Vietnam War on its veterans in the 1980s, which was made into a film. The pond in her life is not a catchment pond like the ones described above, but not exactly unlike a catchment pond, either. It is larger, roughly seventy-five feet long and as wide, and possesses some unusual features. It intercepts the flow of a small stream and overflows into a larger creek after heavy rains. Normally, the two streams are separated by about fifteen feet. Her father wanted "to create a pond for Mama, so that she could go fishing whenever she pleased," Mason writes in *Clear Springs,* a memoir about her family and her search for her own true self. A pond that takes water from a defined stream, however small, and shunts it into another creek in high water might give a pond expert palpitations of the heart. It is an invitation to disaster, and Mason says there have been some. But because the terrain is only mildly rolling, there is not often a heavy runoff into the pond. To bulwark the pond bank so that it would not wash out, Mason's father fortified the levee with heavy rocks. Then, hoping to provide further reinforcement, he dropped an old car that had belonged to her sister into the deep water next to the levee, a refinement of pond technology that has not yet made it into the experts' manuals. Old car hulks would make dandy places for fish to congregate, however. Says Mason, "I'm sure my dad had a fish hotel in mind when he did that."

I first met Bobbie Mason through the pages of the *New Yorker*, in an essay that appeared to be about, of all things, a farm pond. I was surprised that Mason could get an essay about farm ponds published in such a supposedly urbane periodical. But there it was, in the very first sentence, which would turn out to be the very first sentence of *Clear Springs:* "It is late spring, and I am pulling pondweed."

Instantly, all of us pond lovers are hooked. We know all about pulling pondweeds. Mason is actually using the pond to set up the story of her family, especially her mother's story and, even more especially, her own story, but never mind; when a *New Yorker* writer is knee-deep in mud, pulling pondweeds, we want to know why.

As it turned out, Bobbie Mason is something more than a magazine writer. She hails from a small farm in Kentucky, about as far, culturally if not geographically, as one can get from New York. The pond keeps reappearing throughout the book, as Mason tells the story of her struggle to find herself in her family. She wanted to explain a seeming anomaly: that she willingly left the farm but then continued to be drawn back to it. In the very last chapter, the pond becomes a sort of major character in the book, bringing it to a rousing close in a gripping story of how her mother, at age seventy-seven, came dangerously close to death in the pond after she hooked "the old big one," a catfish of monstrous size that she had been after for years. In making sure the fish (thirty-six inches long and probably weighing close to thirty pounds) did not break the line or tear loose from the hook, she grappled with it as she worked it up the pond bank. She lost her balance, slid into the pond, and, determined not to allow the fish to escape, came close to drowning and then to hypothermia. I'll not spoil the story by trying to retell it here, but I was reminded of Santiago in Hemingway's *The Old Man and the Sea* (or Henry Fonda, trying to catch the bass he called "Willard" in the film *On Golden Pond*), transported to what most people would consider a humble little pond on a humdrum little farm, the kind of place where the urban world thinks nothing exciting could ever happen.

I was intrigued to find a novelist—especially one who, by her own admission, wanted to and in fact did leave farm life for the city—beginning and ending her autobiographical book with accounts of the wonders of pasture ponds. When I had the opportunity, I asked her why. She graciously explained in a letter:

> The pond was a very useful metaphor in the book, and my relationship to both the pond and the metaphor are very different from my mother's. She seemed entirely practical about the pond. She worried about the fish and the pondweed and heavy rains and tall grass. But she loved to fish and I think in that pleasure she did have an aesthetic appreciation for the pond, as I did. For me the pond became a focal point of my visits to my parents and the farm. My dad created it in the seventies for my mother to fish in and then he cut down a black walnut tree that was interfering with her view of it from the house. In the book, I looked at the pond through memory and imagination. It was very beautiful. From the banks I could look out at the whole farm, in all directions. The reflections on the surface encompassed the sky and the surrounding encroachments of the modern world—the warehouses, the chicken feed mill, the traffic and highways. On the banks of the pond I knew where I was.

A passage in *Clear Springs* illuminates the significance of the pond as metaphor:

> I had become a writer—belatedly, after many twists and turns while I looked over my shoulder at my childhood dreams and shook my head to get out the nightmare residue from my journey north [to New

York]. I had discovered that I could draw on my true sources in order to write fiction. How could I have failed to recognize them? They had claimed me all along. So much of the culture that I had thought made me inferior turned out to be my wellspring. And my mother was my chief inspiration.

Where she lives now, in another part of Kentucky, she has ponds to enjoy, but "they have little history that I know," she says. "Compared to the pond at home, these are vacant. I have little sense of what they are. I am aware that the water level is always going down. I'm aware of snapping turtles and cattails. One pond, called the cedar pond, is ringed by cedars and is very beautiful. But the water is only three inches deep, sometimes just mud."

Quarter-acre to half-acre hillside catchment ponds are common throughout the foothills of the Appalachians and other hill country where ever-running creeks are few and far between. Some of them were dug large in the first place, but many of them began as seep pools like the one Berry describes. Over the years these seep pools were enlarged to hold more water as the springs began to run only seasonally or dried up completely, so that the pond had to rely on runoff water alone. Sometimes they were enlarged simply to accommodate larger herds of livestock or for fishing.

Where hillsides are big enough and the soil clayey enough to hold water, hillside ponds can be built to rely solely on rainwater. But the placement needs considerable study if no seep spring exists to mark a likely spot. Visualize, for sake of example, the face of a steep hillside perhaps 800 feet long from top to bottom and half that wide, an area of about 320,000 square feet. Roughly that's eight acres. Now visualize building a little pond, say 150 feet in diameter, a cup set into the hillside. Obviously you wouldn't want eight acres of runoff water rushing down a hill into such a pond after a heavy rain. The water would peel the little pond right off the hillside. In such a location, where would you put your catchment pond?

First you study the hillside for a while—several years, anyway. Common sense has already dictated that the pond should be positioned somewhere halfway or more up the slope, not at the bottom, where the velocity of the runoff water would be much greater. So you walk the hillside over and over again, note how the water flows on it, study the folds of the hill for a place where the slope flattens out a little, forming a bit of a shelf upon which to seat the pond. Then you reflect on how you will use the dirt from the catchment to funnel water either into the pond, if you need more watershed, or away from it, if you need less. Where rainfall is normally plentiful, thirty to forty inches per year, two acres or even less of watershed would be sufficient. I know of small ponds that are kept sufficiently filled from a barn roof.

The other important requirement of the hillside pond is that it be dug deep enough so that the downhill bank is almost entirely of undisturbed earth. The reason you want to find a bit of a shelf on the hillside for the pond's location is to avoid the necessity of piling up a large earthen dam on the down side. An earthen dam, built up with newly loosened dirt, could wash out on a steep hillside, even if it had a good clay core in it. For example, Paulandanny's pond, described in chapter 3, is actually a catchment pond on a fairly steep hill, dug into a bit of a levelish shelf halfway down the hill. The downhill side of the pond embankment is very steep, but it is composed of layers of almost solid and undisturbed rock. Even if water should spill over in a very bad rain, very little washing could occur.

I find the contemplation of hillside ponds particularly fascinating, because I plan to build one as soon as time and money become available. My hill is, by Appalachian standards, tiny, maybe 150 feet from top to bottom, but also quite steep. A natural waterway descends this steep little hill from the hayfield above. For years, when this land was mistreated by plowing, that little waterway turned into a gully. The patience of grass has finally healed it. I intend to dig a pond at the foot of the hill, just where that waterway meets level pastureland.

The dirt from the excavation I will pile into two ridges no more than a foot high, fanning out from the pond on either side, diagonally up the hill, so that runoff water will follow the ridges into the pond instead of going straight down the hill. Even on such a small slope, I can gain more than an acre of hillside runoff, at least enough for a pond fifty feet in diameter. I fantasize running at breakneck speed down the hill on a hot haymaking day and, just before reaching the pond, taking a tremendous leap into the air to land like a swan right in the middle of the pond.

PONDS AS SUSTAINING
FOOD CUPBOARDS

Tony Droll was an Ohio farm boy who grew up to be a Franciscan missionary. He then became, by necessity, both a farmer and a missionary in Africa. When he first arrived in his adopted country of Zambia, he was shocked by the meager food supply. The diet of the Lunda tribes he ministered to was critically short of protein, and the resulting malnutrition, he says, "was the major contributor to the sickness that constantly harassed them." With the practiced eye of a farmer, Brother Tony took stock of his surroundings. True, the land was not as rich as an Ohio cornfield, nor the climate as benign for grain and domestic livestock production. But the weather never got nearly as cold in Zambia as in Ohio, either, and there was plenty of water.

He tried to interest the Lunda in various kinds of traditional First World livestock, but, apart from their lack of familiarity with such enterprises, the sources of agricultural supplies they needed were a long distance away. He successfully demonstrated the practicality of raising rabbits at the mission headquarters, but the discipline of husbandry that he had learned on the family farm in Ohio was somewhat foreign to the Lunda, whose tradition rested more on hunting and gathering than on domestic farming. Hunting, however, no longer supplied a constant, reliable source of food, Tony could see, and it was very time-consuming. Moreover, he noticed that the Lunda, given the choice, seemed to prefer fish to meat. As he marveled at the many spring-fed creeks in the area, an idea took root in his mind. It might not be practical to pen up wild animals and raise them, but fish were a different story. Family-sized fishponds might be a practical, user-friendly way for the Lunda to begin supplying themselves with adequate protein.

Information on backyard aquaculture was ten hours away, in the nearest city. So were tilapia fry, the most desirable fish for stocking in the Zambian climate. But he began to experiment. By trial and error, he perfected a pond design that would receive water by gravity from a nearby spring-fed creek through a channel dug between the two. The trick, he learned, was to choose a site where there was a discernible slope downstream from where the channel exited the creek—enough of a grade to gain adequate head or height in the channel, so that the water could fill a pond to a depth of two to three feet and then flow back into the stream, all by gravity. Any gentle slope close to an ever-running stream that could keep a pond three feet deep at its lower end and about a foot deep at the upper end made a good site. On the best sites more than one pond could be dug, side by side, all fed by the same channel from the creek. The wall or dam at the deep end required a slope of about three to one so it wouldn't leak. Allowing for a top width of at least a yard for a convenient walkway for seining the pond, that meant a dam about five yards wide at the bottom. The side walls were, of course, about that size at the lower end of the pond and then gradually tapered smaller back to the upper end.

All that dirt had to be dug and moved by excruciatingly slow and arduous hand labor, with hoes, shovels, and wheelbarrows. The essential clay core or key inside the base of the walls he dug a foot wide and a foot deep and filled with impervious clay. The clay had to be tamped solid, by hand. In fact, all the dirt had to be tamped or pounded routinely by hand as the earthen walls went up. There was also the channel from the creek to dig, by hand, and it had to be equipped with some kind of water gate so that the flow into the pond was not greater than what the outlet pipe could handle. Some water had to flow constantly through the pond to keep it full and to provide supplemental oxygen.

Tony's ponds varied in size from thirty-five by twenty yards up to eighty-five by fifty yards. His seine stretched fifty-five yards, so the width of the ponds had to be less than that. The largest he built were eighty-five yards by fifty yards, more than adequate for a family's needs. "I would think that a pond ought not to be less than fifteen yards by ten yards to be practical," he says. "The bigger ones I built were more productive per square yard than the smaller ones."

Once construction was complete, he scattered pig and poultry manure and agricultural lime over the bottom to stimulate plankton growth. "But no sawdust or wood chips mixed in the manure," he warns. "That can make the water too acid."

Within a few days after filling, the water turned greenish with plant plankton, which in turn encouraged zooplankton. "If you stick your hand into the water an arm's length, and you can just barely see your fingers, you've got the plankton population about right. If you can't see your fingers, there's too much plankton; if you can see them very plainly, too little."

Then he made the ten-hour trip to get tilapia fry to stock the pond. "I put them in plastic bags partially full of water and pumped the bags full of air with a bicycle pump. I'd stop every hour or so and pump in more air. About half the fish survived." Eventually, he stocked carp, too. The carp and tilapia complemented each other.

"The most important part of fish management is feeding," he says. "Fish can actually survive in well-oxygenated water on very limited nourishment drawn through their gills. But they need plenty of feed to grow fast enough for a dependable food supply." Feeding commercial, balanced rations was out of the question for families in rural Africa. The feed would have been too expensive, even if available. Lacking grain wastes from a mill, which he figured might have made a suitable supplement, he fed manure from chickens, rabbits, and pigs. The liquid manure enhanced water quality, and the solid particles fell to the bottom, where the fish ate them. Table scraps and unused garden vegetables he chopped into small pieces for the fish. He also fed compost. "We achieved a sort of circular system where the manures from the animals went to the garden and to the fish. When the fishpond was drained for repair work, the sludge from the bottom made ideal fertilizer for the garden. In a sense, the garden, the animals and the fish all fed the people while feeding each other."

While fishing in a river one day, Brother Tony discovered another way to provide supplemental fish food in the ponds. "We were trolling for bream, and when we got a good strike at a certain spot in the river, we turned the boat around and went back to it. Sure enough, another big bream. Passing back and forth over the spot, we caught five, and I was curious why that was so. Then I noticed a dead water monitor in the tree directly above the spot where we were catching the fish. Maggots were dropping from it into the water there." When he got back to the mission pond, he built a vented platform of small forest poles out over the water, put a dead animal on it, and waited for the maggots. "The fish thought this was a great idea," he says. He began the habit of commandeering animal carcasses he came across and using them for maggot production over the pond. Says another missionary, Bryan Hoban, who worked with Tony for many years: "Nothing is wasted in Zambia. If you dump a load of what Americans would call trash along a road, it will be all gone by the next morning."

"But when I suggested to local fish farmers that they utilize dead dogs this way, they absolutely refused," remarks Brother Tony, with his habitual playful grin. Why? "They said that if fish ate the maggots dropping off the dead dog, and the people ate the fish, that would the same as eating the dog. Eating dog was taboo. No amount of explanation that the maggot was the larva of the fly would convince them otherwise. So back to the drawing boards." He built a wooden box over the water with a gangplank to the dam so he could push wheelbarrows full of pig manure to the box. After a few hot days, the maggots became well established in the manure and were contributing nicely to the fish below the platform. This was more acceptable to the people. "But few of them had enough animals to carry out such an operation," says Tony.

The natives marveled at Tony's work but were slow to respond. Finally a man by the name of Mbimbi, who had helped build the first pond, decided that he wanted one too. The mission supplied tools and two wheelbarrows. Mbimbi dug while his two wives manned the wheelbarrows. His children carried dirt in big slabs of bark on their heads. The family kept at it steadily except during bouts of malaria. After the pond filled, Mbimbi cleverly regulated inflow by the number of rocks he placed in the channel. Brother Tony supplied stockfish from the mission pond. Mbimbi's children carried fish from the mission pond to stock their new one a kilometer away. They ran the whole distance to make sure the oxygen in the buckets did not become depleted. The family celebrated with a calabash of honey beer. Says Brother Tony, "I had hooked my first fish."

A second man, Kafupi, decided to build. Again the mission supplied tools and know-how. Again the seine was pulled through the mission pond and again the children ran through the bush carrying the fish in buckets to the new pond. Says Tony, "I had hooked my second fish."

But still there was hesitancy in the community. "We learned that many people were convinced that they would have to pay the missionaries for their help and return some of the fish when their ponds started producing," says Tony. "When they realized that was not true, the dam of skepticism broke. Ponds started going in everywhere."

War in Angola sent refugees fleeing into Zambia. The food supply, already barely adequate, became critical. "The United Nations High Commission for Refugees was called to work in cooperation with the church to bring relief," says Tony. "Their solution to the crisis was truckloads and planes-full of food staples. That was a temporary and short-term solution. Many refugees would not even come out of the bush for the food, for fear the UN would send them back to Angola to face their death. I started talking about my fishponds. The UN was so impressed that it started providing funds and help. We received hundreds of wheelbarrows and shovels. We could hire supervisors and diggers. I could start fish-farming training programs. Many ponds were built in a short time. The UN brought in fish to stock the ponds in ten-ton aerated tankers. All in all, two thousand ponds were built."

Although many of the ponds are still used as intended, the success story is, as Tony puts it, "speckled." As so often happens with new aquacultural programs everywhere, some practitioners lost heart and gave up for a variety of reasons. Thieves were a constant plague, in the form not only of predatory crocodiles, otters, and water monitors, but of humans. The careful husbandry involved in successful fish farming discouraged some families. Once again, experience suggested that introduced changes take a long time to become a habitual part of a culture. If we Americans had a long tradition of cleaning our teeth by chewing road tar (which works quite effectively), I wonder how readily we would adopt brushes and toothpaste at the insistence of an outsider.

But Tony had planted an idea. Family-sized aquaculture continues to this day. "It is not uncommon now to see dried, smoked, and salt-cured fish for sale on the side of the road, a sight that was not to be observed previously unless the dried fish were ferried from Angola by bicycle," he says.

And Tony goes on planting new ideas. His latest project in Zambia is a school and home for hundreds of children orphaned by disease, war, and malnutrition. You should hear them sing.

Another "Missionary"

In the United States, one of the most noteworthy pioneers of home fish production was Bob Rodale, the famed head of Rodale Press until his untimely death in 1990. He was one of the most independent thinkers that I've had the privilege of knowing well. One of the most memorable conversations (for me anyway) that I had with him took place in a vegetarian restaurant. Neither of us was vegetarian, but both of us were willing to consider everything. He had just started a new farm magazine, and we were discussing whether we should encourage horse farming, which seemed to be the thing a contrarian magazine about farming ought to do. I was a bit surprised when Bob did not appear particularly enthusiastic. "I've been talking to Ivan Illich [the extremely contrary Jesuit philosopher and educator]," he explained. "Ivan was horrified at the idea of using beasts to power farm equipment. He says until food is once again the product of an advanced technology based on human labor, we have not solved the inherent problem of energy." Bob paused then and dared me, with his eyes, to disagree. When I only smiled, he did too. "You have to admit," he said, "Ivan is onto something there."

Bob believed that the backyard pond was a logical and practical counterpart to the backyard garden. Impressed by the reports coming out of China about the prodigious amount of protein that oriental farmers could produce from a combination of aquaculture and agriculture, he wrote in 1971 that the whole world "must learn to walk through the water." He saw a new frontier in food production, "growing a variety of plants with aquatic and amphibian animals in a series of ponds on a small homestead." His vision is coming true. Les Brown, of the renowned Worldwatch Institute, wrote in the April 2001 issue of *American Small Farm* that "fish farming is poised to overtake cattle ranching as a food source by the end of this decade."

In addition to funding aquacultural research at other institutions, Rodale was able, in 1976, to begin his own serious experimentation. A backyard pool and a farm pond were constructed at his farm. Later, he purchased another small mountainside property blessed with springs for aquacultural experiments. Unfortunately, this work was more or less discontinued after his death.

But while it lasted, Rodale and his staff evolved completely combined agri-aquacultural food production systems that are still very much applicable to the backyard and homestead. The most novel experiment I saw was feeding chickens in cages over small constructed ponds, so that the hens' manure fell into the water and provided the fish with food, following similar practices in Asian countries. I was working for Rodale Press at the time and was fascinated when I saw this experiment in operation. It really worked. Eventually it was discontinued because objections were raised against keeping chickens in cages. That problem could easily have been solved by building small chicken coops next to the ponds, with the roosting area extending out over the water. Knowing Bob, I'm sure he would have been the first to advocate this solution once the idea of feeding fish on chicken waste was proven practical. Chickens do most of their defecating while roosting, so the fish would have gotten fed, and during the day the hens could go about their normal routine in an otherwise traditional coop or outdoors.

Homer Buck at the Parr Fisheries Research Center near Kinmundy, Illinois, was at that time also experimenting with feeding fish with manure. He had visited China, where the practice is many centuries old. In his experiments pigs were fed grain rations on concrete, and the manure was washed directly into ponds for carp, catfish, and other fish. Gains of catfish and bass were negligible, Buck reported, but gains of the various kinds of carp were remarkable. Not only that, but the carp purified the water, keeping it above EPA standards for clean water.

Another of Rodale's experiments involved a series of small pools adjacent to the experimental gardens at his farm. The goal was to see if each such pond would produce just fifty pounds of cleaned fish, increasing a family's food supply by about as much as a dozen chickens or rabbits. How small could such a pond be? What equipment would be necessary? Could the fish be fed on pond life, kitchen scraps, and other home sources of protein?

Channel catfish, buffalo fish, and mirror carp (also called Israeli carp, a selected strain of common carp) were stocked in six pools, each twelve feet in diameter and three feet deep. These species were chosen because they were easily available to homeowners. The buffalo fish proved rather unsatisfactory, mostly because they were not as readily available as had been anticipated and had to be shipped in from far away. But the catfish and carp performed quite well, and the experiment was considered a success. It certainly impressed me. Six ponds, tanks actually, about ten feet in diameter and two feet deep, were dug and lined with plastic, and the water was fertilized with one and one-half pounds of hog manure in each pond. After an algal bloom was established, the ponds were stocked: twenty catfish fingerlings in three of them and ten mirror carp in the other three. Ten buffalo fish were stocked in each of the six ponds. The catfish were fed a commercial trout ration. The carp and buffalo ate table scraps and algae.

Caring for the fish was not demanding but did require daily attention. Most of the time went into learning about water quality and cultivating a healthy colony of algae for oxygen production, fish food, and water purification. At the start, water was tested regularly for pH, temperature, ammonia, and oxygen. Of these, only oxygen levels became critical enough to merit constant checks. With a little experience researchers learned to gauge oxygen levels by the color of the algae and by the weather.

Because photosynthesis stops at night, the pools had to make do on what oxygen accumulated during the day, which is not a problem in a natural environment. Because there were substantial variations between pools in algal growth, the researchers used an aerator in each for backup oxygen. Oxygen levels were very good for the first half of the season. In late August and September, however, long stretches of cloudy days coupled with cooling weather didn't support enough photosynthesis to maintain adequate oxygen for the steadily growing fish. It was found necessary to have pools that did not leak, because adding water constantly severely disrupted algal growth.

Feeding the fish took only minutes a day. Table scraps were blended according to a rule-of-thumb formula using 50 percent high-protein scraps, 25 percent green vegetable matter, and 25 percent high-carbohydrate foods, all run through a food grinder. The fish were fed according to what they would take. Occasional weight checks on these amounts provided an indication of how much they had grown.

By late October the water had cooled so that the fish weren't eating much, and the pools were harvested. The late start had reduced the ideal season by about 25 percent, and periods of low oxygen had inhibited growth. Still, the pools produced fish of edible size. Overall conversion was about two pounds of feed to one of fish.

The catfish grew especially well, averaging almost a pound each at harvest. The carp averaged one and one-half pounds. The handful of surviving buffalo reached a little over half a pound apiece. Comparing these weight gains to the amount of feed given on an equal dry-matter basis showed that the table scraps nourished the fish as well as the commercial trout feed did.

Water from the ponds was used to irrigate a nearby vegetable plot. At the end of the season, the nutrient-rich fish water had boosted yields in that plot 35 percent higher than in an identical garden watered directly from a spring.

Rodale researchers also tried to grow fish in cages in large existing bodies of water. From a practical point of view, cage culturing of fish has some disadvantages, because the fish must be fed nearly their entire diet. But cages have some advantages, especially for the home producer who lives next to a larger river or lake. Even in a farm pond, especially if it is a large one, cage culture might be more convenient and timesaving (depending on one's purposes, surely not mine) than trying to seine the fish or using hook and line. Also, fish that would multiply too fast in the pond might be raised in a cage in the pond if the water watcher was extremely careful not to let any fish escape to the pond. Since cage production is more closely linked with commercial aquaculture, a subject a bit beyond the scope of this book, I will not go into detail. But the experiment is interesting enough at least to describe briefly.

The experimenters built their own cages of high-density black polyethylene netting, which is practically indestructible, over wooden frames. Each cage measured a cubic yard and was topped by a Styrofoam float. In the first attempt the cages were stocked late, July 11, and harvested October 7. Growth rates were highly encouraging, however, with catfish increasing in weight on the average from 50 grams to 83 grams and bluegills, in another cage, from 45 grams to 116 grams. (It takes 28.35 grams to make an ounce. Researchers think that they sound more impressive if they use the metric system, and in this case it makes the increase in weight sound more impressive. I hate the metric system.) However, most of the bluegills were lost when the wind blew their cage over. Another problem was that muskrats in the farm pond gnawed on the Styrofoam floats.

This pioneering project did not turn out very successfully, and that should be a word to the wise. Today, however, much, much more is known about cage production, and information and supplies are available from all aquacultural supply companies. In my tramping territory, Freshwater Farms of Ohio, near Urbana, is a leader in—and does consulting work about—the development of cage production in larger bodies of water, especially old stone quarry lakes where the water is unpolluted.

Solar Greenhouse Fishponds

Backyard fish growers have tried many variations of the pioneering work done at the New Alchemy Institute in the 1970s. Basically, a garden pool is roofed in double layers of plastic or fiberglass, turning it into a greenhouse. Some earlier experiments used a geodesic dome design, because geodesic domes were all the rage then. Other designs of passive solar greenhouses will work well, too. Sunlight coming through the roof or windows in cold weather warms the water, which stores the heat for nighttime use. The warmth increases algal growth for the fish. The algae help oxygenate the water, but in many instances small electric pumps also help oxygenate and circulate the water through filters to keep it clean. Bob Huke, a professor at Dartmouth, took the idea further. In a greenhouse that was heated only by the sun, he and his wife, Ellie, raised catfish in summer, trout in winter, and fresh vegetables nine months a year. The tank of water in the center of the greenhouse acted as a heat sink for incoming sunlight, releasing the stored warmth at night and on cloudy days, and water temperatures stayed high enough in winter that the trout remained active. The fish, in turn, enriched the water with their wastes, and the water could be used to irrigate and fertilize the vegetables.

Around the outer perimeter of the greenhouse structure, three-inch-thick sheets of foam insulation extended four feet into the ground. This insulation prevented winter loss of soil heat to the frozen ground outside. The southern, eastern, and western exposures were initially covered with ten-mil plastic film stapled to the outside. This proved too flimsy, and the plastic was replaced with sturdier fiberglass. The north-facing wall was covered with one-and-a-half-inch foam insulation board with aluminum foil on the inside to reflect the sun's rays. The water tank measured six by twelve feet on the sides and was thirty-four inches deep—it was actually the bottom half of a prefab concrete two-thousand-gallon septic tank.

Water in the tank circulated through a filter made of two connected fifty-five-gallon drums filled with a matrix of plastic rings (available from aquacultural supply houses). Water was pumped through the filter and aerated by dropping from the top of the second drum in a cascade back into the tank. Water temperature rose to as high as ninety degrees Fahrenheit in summer, which the catfish didn't mind, and in winter fell only to a low of thirty-five degrees, which the trout could tolerate. The Hukes put about seventy-five catfish fingerlings in the fourteen-hundred-gallon tank on April 15 and harvested them on November 15 at an average weight of three-quarters of a pound. A dozen or so trout were stocked in the pond within a week after the catfish were gone. When harvested in spring, they averaged twelve and a half inches long—from five inches initial stocking size.

The catfish ate algae, fish scraps, and a commercial trout feed. The trout fattened almost exclusively on commercial feed. Bob Huke said that he could have bought his fish cheaper, but when he added in the quality of the food, the entertainment value of the project, and the many years the pool and the greenhouse should last, the venture was profitable enough.

Trout in Concrete Pools

I must thank Jan Michalek, now deceased, for the best trout I've ever eaten. He was a most original and independent person, which is to say that he could be on occasion cantankerous and contrary. In the latter part of his life, when raising trout in backyard concrete pools became an obsession with him, he managed to irritate or alienate just about every other trout expert in Ohio, especially Ohio State University scientists. "They won't believe my method works even when they see it working," he railed at me when I visited him. He loved to tell the tale of sending a graduate student into his garden to get some potatoes; she came back empty-handed because she didn't know they were under the ground.

Michalek came to Ohio from his native Czechoslovakia as a political refugee. His working background was in fish management and production. When he saw the numerous springs of southern Ohio he was ecstatic. "Every farm or backyard with a good spring can be a dependable source of the finest fish supply in the world," he said. Wildlife biologists scoffed. When Michalek claimed he could raise a thousand pounds of trout in a thousand gallons of water, they were as incredulous as the scientists of another day had been when told what Galileo's telescope had revealed. So Michalek started building trout ponds like those he knew about in Czechoslovakia. His concrete, or sometimes gunite, ponds were circular dishes, measuring sixteen feet in diameter, holding ten inches of water on the outer edge and thirty inches in the center. Springwater entered through a pipe at the outer edge, spilled over a baffle board, and fell into the pond. At the center, the water drained out of a standpipe through a special filter designed to empty water at the same flow rate as it entered the pool. The design of the pool, and the way the water flowed through it, caused the water to swirl very slowly. The moving water was one of the keys, Michalek always said, to the success of his densely populated ponds. "Trout like moving water."

He was most insistent upon what he called the key factor to success with his pool design. "You must have a flow rate from the spring of ten to fifteen gallons per minute for *one* pool. If you get greedy and try to run two pools with that amount of water, or if you try to make your pool bigger than the sixteen-foot diameter I use, you will run into trouble. If you want two pools, you have to have a flow rate of eighteen to twenty-five gallons per minute." (Incidentally, and this applies to any kind of spring-fed pond where flow rate is important to the design, make sure you measure flow rate in periods of the least flow. If you design for a flow rate in springtime and the flow rate declines in the fall, you could be in trouble.)

The only problem I ever heard of with a Michalek pond was a case where water froze in the standpipe filter and the wind knocked it over, causing fish to wash out the drain to the ground below the pool.

Nevertheless, none of these little commercial trout ponds are still in operation, as far as I know. As with Brother Tony's ponds and Bob Rodale's agri-aquaculture experiments, the work is constant and sophisticated enough that it requires the devotion of a traditional husbandman, a rarity today. Perfectly good, workable ideas await a time when backyard fish production becomes as common a part of our heritage as gardening.

Fish in a Downspout Barrel

Simpler methods must first become routine in the backyard. For example, some gardeners have tried raising fish in rather small, plastic-lined tanks. I know of one experimenter in Alabama who stocked forty fingerling catfish in a standard fifty-five-gallon barrel under the downspout of his roof. He fed them first on commercial catfish feed and then almost entirely on fish worms that he was also raising. (His account of his experience appeared in the November 1973 issue of *Organic Gardening and Farming*.) For the extra oxygen that such a system would need, he used an aquarium bubbler and a hose in the barrel that siphoned off fifteen gallons of water a day to be replaced by fresh water. The old water was used to irrigate a garden and compost worm bins next to the barrel. The worms were fed to the fish. Table scraps were fed to the worms. The fish were so enthusiastic for the worms that when the grower approached the barrel, they would have leaped right out were it not for the glass pane he had put over the barrel. The experimenter's only water source was chlorinated city water, so he let it sit in the sun in buckets so that some of the chlorine escaped before the water was added to the barrel.

The channel catfish proved to be unusually efficient food producers; a one-pound fish yielded approximately ten ounces of meat. Fish fed on either commercial fish rations or worms converted about 85 percent of their food to meat.

The most important variable was water temperature. Catfish will feed at temperatures as low as forty to forty-five degrees Fahrenheit, but their greatest growth was achieved at eighty-four degrees. So the experimenter painted the barrel black and moved it to full sun. He reported a decided increase in feeding activity. Although summer growth was greatest, the catfish grew adequately in the relatively mild winters of Alabama.

Care had to be taken not to overfeed in such a small body of water. In warm water and bright sunlight, any uneaten worms would die and decompose rapidly, giving off gases that could be poisonous to the fish.

Learning from a Horse Tank

I know all the ideas described above are workable because, when I was a child, we kept minnows and catfish in the concrete horse tank in the barnyard year round, with no care at all except the fun of feeding them bread crumbs and worms. I think the main purpose of the minnows was to have a handy source of bait when Dad wanted to go fishing, which was often. My grandfather had a notion that the minnows kept mosquitoes from breeding in the tank, which was probably true. The tank measured four by eight feet, and about four feet deep, about half the depth below soil level. A low roof extended over half of the tank, and the roof was covered with about a foot of sawdust. The sawdust provided enough insulation that the intake valve rarely froze, although the water surface at the open end of the tank often did. Because the animals drank from the tank, there was a daily influx of new water from the wooden water-storage tank under the windmill at the well, and I guess that the movement of water from well to storage tank to horse tank, plus the algae that grew on the walls of the tank, brought enough oxygen for the minnows and the catfish. Catfish not only thrived, but one of them hatched out a brood. I watched with great fascination the little black cloud of catfish fry hovering in the water. Those tiny fish would follow the water pipes to the stock-watering tank behind the barn, and in the other direction they managed the almost unbelievable feat of swimming upstream in the pipes and ending up in the toilet bowl in the new indoor bathroom! My mother did not think this was as funny as the rest of us did.

I have very distinct memories of that horse tank, not only because of my mother's fussing about catfish in the toilet bowl, but because she worried that we would drown in it. The horse tank was one of our favorite toys. We floated toy boats driven by rubber band–powered paddles on it. We fished for the catfish with varying luck. Occasionally we were allowed to "swim" in it, although it was a mighty small swimming pool. One day when I was monkeying with the oilcan, a drop of oil spilled on the surface of the water. I was transfixed with the beautiful colors that spread slowly out from the droplet. Until Dad thought I was overdoing it, I would let the oil drip and then watch, with my nose almost touching the water surface, as every color of the spectrum drifted out into the surrounding water. Nothing on television years later seemed as wondrous.

The horse tank was also the scene of my first scientific experiment. My cousins had told me that horsehair snakes actually come from horsehairs. It has always been difficult to get me to believe anything that sounds like nonsense, which leaves me today with fewer friends than I might have. But, well, what did I really know about horsehair snakes? So I pulled some hairs out of Flora's mane and threw them into the tank. Believe it or not, several weeks later there were some horsehair snakes wriggling in the water. The experiment taught me the best scientific lesson of all: the results of experiments aren't always to be trusted.

Bullfrogs for Frog Legs

Fish are not the only food that humans could depend on from their ponds. In fact, when I think of the huge supply of potential food that is all around us, I wonder how there can be so many undernourished people in the climate of the United States. What tragic stupidity has overtaken our educational system?

Bullfrogs, from which come that expensive restaurant delicacy, frog legs, are overpopulating our little pond, and we did nothing consciously to make this happen. Just build it, and they will come. In case you wonder if bullfrogs have yet taken up residence in your pond, listen. Their "song" is unmistakable. You will think there is a bull down in the water, emitting stentorian moans. You can spear the frogs rather easily at night by flashlight. Sometimes you can catch them on fishhooks baited with worms or even a bit of red cloth. Our bullfrogs are so tame that I could catch them with a fishnet. For a winter treat, dig a hole in the shallows of a pond, maybe two feet deep and a foot in diameter. The soft mud that settles on the bottom of natural ponds will settle especially in the hole. Bullfrogs like to hibernate in that mud if it gets deep enough to cover them well. Then in winter cut a hole in the ice over the hole, if necessary, and scoop out the frogs. I haven't yet tried that myself, but that's what the old-timers say. (Now that I am fast becoming an old-timer myself, I wonder how many old-timers pass along gems of folklore that they have never tried.)

To skin a frog, make an incision down the back and then peel the skin down the legs with a pair of pliers. Keep the frog wet beforehand and it will skin easier. Also, if the frog dries out, the meat tends to lose flavor in a hurry. A good way to prepare frog legs is to powder them with flour, dip in egg batter, dust lightly with cracker meal, and place in vegetable oil preheated to 400 degrees Fahrenheit until the legs begin to brown. Then reduce the temperature to 375 and fry the legs as you would chicken.

In the South a bullfrog can mature in six months or less. In the North, figure on two years. In an enclosed system where some form of artificial heating is used, the northern frog might be forced to grow as fast as the southern, but at a rather high cost. A few frogs could be raised even in a garden pool, if you surrounded it with a fence at least four feet high and of a small enough mesh so the frogs could not escape. The water needs to be only six inches deep. In such a situation the frogs would probably eat some of their own tadpoles, which is okay. There will likely be too many for a small pool anyway. Bullfrogs, by the way, may stay in the tadpole stage for a whole year in the North.

Canada Goose Sandwiches

Even the most wildly loyal lover of wildlife will admit today that Canada geese have overpopulated into a bad problem, partially because of the proliferation of farm and park ponds. There are too many geese because, especially in urban areas, they have few pre-dators, and ignorant human laws protect them from hunting. But slowly society is getting over that kind of ignorance. If geese are ruining your pond, and you have enlightened laws in your area, eat some of them. It is difficult to tell young ones from old ones, but the younger, the better. If you have allowed the geese to nest around your pond, you can usually tell which are the young ones just off the nest, because they are smaller.

Anyway, an acquaintance of mine who is blessed with a fairly large pond right off his backyard tells me that goose sandwiches are deli-cious. He cooks a goose this way: Line pan with aluminum foil. Place cleaned goose in pan stuffed with an apple and a big onion. Pour half a bottle of wine (port preferred) over the goose and seal up the goose and wine in the foil. Cook at 325 degrees for thirty minutes per pound of goose. Sealing the bird in the foil is the secret, he says. It keeps the meat moist.

For sandwiches he puts cranberry sauce on the meat. That's a new one to me.

Kentucky Fried Snapping Turtle and Roasted Muskrat

Build a pond, and turtles, like frogs, will come—and they will make themselves quite at home. One of my sisters and her husband live right next to their pond. She was startled one morning to find two snappers in her garden! They were laying eggs and burying them between the pea rows.

Of the several very palatable species, the snapping turtle is the best adapted to warm-water farm ponds. In fact, the increase in artificial ponds has been the salvation of the snapping turtle in the Midwest, even if not necessarily the salvation of my sister's garden. When I was young, snappers had become somewhat rare here because of human predation. The meat is very good: dark meat in the four legs and tail and white meat in the neck. Catching one in your garden or any other place on land is very simple. Just step on the carapace to bring it to a halt and pick it up by the tail. But be careful. Snappers bite viciously, and their necks are about twice as long as they appear to be tucked up under the carapace. To catch turtles in the creek when I was a boy, I set lines of strong cord and large fishhooks baited with the carcasses of English sparrows that I had shot with my air rifle, and good riddance.

I've on occasion caught a snapper by reaching stealthily into the pond and just grabbing it by the tail. Or I have waded ponds and creeks with a steel rod, poking down through mud and debris and waterweeds where I suspected that snappers were lurking. When the rod hits a turtle carapace, there's an unusual thunking sound. Step on the turtle's back. Slide your hand down your boot and gingerly locate the edge of the carapace. This is called living dangerously—but not really. The shell of the snapper has a few jagged points toward the back (away from the jaws), and there is a hollow under the edge of the shell at the back legs. These signs guide your hand to the turtle's tail and not his head. Only the experienced should do this, but how do you get experience?

Commercial production of freshwater turtles is not commonly practiced, but snapping turtles can be raised easily in captivity. Our son had one in an aquarium in his room for three years. He fed it hamburger and fish worms, but its rate of growth was very slow.

We never have made turtle soup, considering fried turtle meat much more scrumptious. Cut the heads off and hang the turtles by the tail, so the blood drains out well. Turtles often have leeches affixed to them and may otherwise reek of the stagnant water that they don't mind living in. A huge snapper was once captured in the Cuyahoga River near Cleveland when the river was so polluted with oil that it caught fire.

To butcher, lay the decapitated turtle upside down on its shell, cut around the undershell, or plastron, and lift it out. Next, peel off the skin with a pair of pliers. Then cut out the six pieces: neck, tail, and four legs. There is another strip of meat on the underside of the top shell, behind a latticework of little bones. These bones must be broken to get out the meat, which we always called tenderloin. Because the tenderloin is difficult to remove and not very large at that, we usually didn't bother.

We used to soak the meat overnight in salt water, though I have heard other turtle fanciers say brine soaking is unnecessary. In the morning we browned the meat after rolling it in cornmeal, then fried it as you would southern fried chicken.

Large snappers can pull a baby duck under water as it swims by and drown it. If you have any prize ducklings or goslings, you might pause a little before putting them on a pond known to contain large snappers. The turtles will not harm swimmers in farm ponds—at least I've never heard of that happening. But the shark-fear psychosis engendered by recent news events unfortunately has induced some farm pond owners to try to get rid of their snapping turtles.

Muskrats provide a palatable and healthful meat. Because "rat" is part of their name, most people shudder at the idea of eating them. ("Musk" doesn't sound very tasty either.) But they have beautiful fur and eat a clean, vegetarian diet. Since they invariably populate (and invariably threaten to overpopulate) farm ponds, harvesting them for the table should be encouraged. Cook them as you would young groundhog, which is to say, as you would fried or baked chicken.

I have not been able to get wild rice or cranberries to grow in my pond, but these plants are definitely possibilities for pond gardeners where climate and water pH are appropriate. Cranberries require very acid soil: that's why they are often found in upland bogs. In northern Minnesota, home of wild rice, I have heard of using dynamite to blow open a bit of clear water in a marsh for wild rice production. Instant food pond! But perhaps the most imaginative idea yet comes from Florida, where water hyacinth often chokes the waterways. Thinking ecologically, scientists at the University of Florida asked themselves what could, or would, eat vast quantities of the weed. Answer: water buffalo. Again, this seems ludicrous to us because we are accustomed to cows, pigs, and chickens as our chief meat animals. The water buffaloes that the university used (from a zoo in Canada) grew just fine on water hyacinth and could be a fine source of meat. But such ideas don't fit human social lifestyles, at least in First World countries. That could change. Who would ever have thought that alligator farms would come to commercial agriculture?

PONDS AND SUSTAINABLE
TECHNOLOGY

In 1991, in a visit to an unusual wastewater treatment facility in Indiana, I experienced a profound change in my thinking about shit. I lost my revulsion for human feces. I was looking at an experiment in turning "sewage" into clean water using only biological methods. Jim Davis, the creator of the comic strip "Garfield," had decided to establish the new headquarters of his company, Paws, Incorporated, out in the countryside near his hometown of Fairmont, Indiana (you *can* go home again), where it would have beneficial financial impact on a rural area that needed it. But the location was far from a city sewer line to serve his three big office buildings. He turned the problem into an opportunity. Using methods pioneered by John Todd and his Ocean Arks International organization in Falmouth, Massachusetts, he asked engineers to design a wastewater treatment plant that in actuality would be a solar food- and fiber-producing greenhouse. Among purposes other than the immediate one of cleaning the wastewater so it could flow back into natural waterways, Davis wanted a place to raise tree seedlings and ornamental plants. One of the lesser-known projects of this remarkable cartoonist was buying old farms and returning them to some semblance of their original, natural state.

Standing in the "greenhouse," I could hardly believe what I was seeing. Wastewater that had been pumped first through a grinder and then into a holding tank, where some of the waste settled out and was composted, was flowing slowly into and through a series of tanks and little artificial pools, where it was being purified by water plants and animals. With my nose almost literally up against the first clear fiberglass tank into which wastewater flowed, bodily waste appeared no longer as a brown mass of smelly crud, but as cloudy water with only a trace of odor, in which individual food particles floated. Corn and tomatoes had been high on the office workers' menus recently, because the kernels and seeds were much in evidence. But I felt more like I was peering into a big test tube in a laboratory, not a septic tank.

Sunlight streaming through this giant test tube, and five others just like it, activated the growth of algae. Grease-eating bacteria and nitrifying bacteria that had been introduced to the tank, along with many other bacteria present naturally, were working with the algae to begin the purification process. The nitrifying bacteria "ate" the ammonia, and the subsequent nitrates were "eaten" by the algae and by water hyacinths on the water surface. Snails were eating the algae. The surplus growth of water hyacinth was removed periodically and composted. Air blown through standard garden drip hose in the bottom of the tank bubbled upward, raising the amount of oxygen in the water. Outgoing, cleaner water rose from the bottom of the tank through a standpipe and flowed into the next tank by gravity.

In a second stage of purification, the plant and animal populations in the fiberglass tanks were higher, especially of snails and algae. "I just threw into the tank a couple of handfuls of native snails from ponds in the area, and their population exploded," said Russ Vernon, the horticulturist in charge of the operation.

Going into the third stage of purification, the water, which was constantly aerated to keep the process aerobic, was clean enough to support bluegills. They fed on the snails. The "waste" water was then pumped across the aisle into the "lagoon" phase of the treatment process. The ammonia content, said Vernon, had by now been reduced from some twenty-five to fifty parts per million to five to ten parts per million. The lagoon was approximately two and a half feet deep, four feet wide, and twenty feet long. Sodium vapor lights overhead provided supplemental light and heat for the plants growing in it. The lagoon was kept aerated too, like the tanks, by air bubbling through drip hose. On the water surface more water hyacinths grew, plus arrowhead, duckweed, and black willow tree seedlings on floats. The tree seedlings had very vigorous root systems. "We tried water lilies," said Vernon, "but they did not do well in our somewhat turbulent, aerated water. Water lilies prefer still water." Four kinds of fish swam in the lagoon: koi, tropical sucker fish (*Placastema*), mosquito fish (*Gambusia*), and bluegills.

From the lagoon the treated water was pumped back across the aisle to a small artificial wetland marsh, built up from two and a half feet of egg-sized stones overlaid with six inches of pea gravel. Water stood in part of the marsh, while in other sections it lay just beneath the surface. A timer operated an electric valve that directed water from the lagoon for twenty-four hours to one side of the little "marsh" and then for twenty-four hours to the other side. The marsh was physically divided into two sections by the plastic liner. Standpipes controlled the water level on either side of the marsh.

Over this little artificial wetland, dragonflies darted. In it grew elephant ear, reed canary grass, bulrushes, papyrus, wild aster, monkey flowers, variegated orchard grass, Japanese blood grass, wild iris, calladium, smartweed, and angel trumpet, a flower of surpassing beauty. "It gives off a fragrance at night that I can often still smell when I arrive in the morning," said Vernon. "I wanted to stick to native Indiana wetland plants, but many of them go dormant in winter, so I've added temperate and tropical plants to assure year-round growth. I am now starting to experiment with orchids."

The water was retained in the system for five days, twice as long as a standard treatment plant. Water coming out of the marsh splashed over a venturi aeration device for further aeration before exiting into a pipe that carried it to a natural waterway. In summer the water was sterilized with ultraviolet light to remove any trace of human disease pathogens still remaining. "Yes, I suppose we could drink the water at this point," said Vernon, smiling. "But no one does."

The water was, nevertheless, remarkably clean. According to the tests Vernon was doing, the ammonia content was lower than that of the distilled water he used as a check. "We don't have any heavy metals to worry about, but if we did, there are tree seedlings we could use to take them out of the water, and then we could plant the seedlings and hold the heavy metal content out of the food chain for forty years or more—until science knows what to do with them."

No chemicals were being added to the system. "The only thing we put in the water is a little baking soda, which provides carbon for the bacteria to eat," said Vernon. "We easily met the effluent standards for carbonaceous biochemical oxygen demand (CBOD), total suspended solids (TTSS), *E. coli* count, pH, and dissolved oxygen."

About a decade later, in 2000, Oberlin College in northern Ohio installed a somewhat similar but even more astounding water purification system in a new building that houses the Environmental Studies Program. The Adam Joseph Lewis Center, as it is called, is a triumph of environmental science. Through the latest advances in solar paneling, it generates much of its own electricity. On days when there is a surplus, it is sold back into the public utility grid. If or when electric blackouts start rolling across Ohio, students in the center may not know it until they leave the building. Wastewater is purified and recycled back to the flush toilets in the restrooms. Building materials emphasize recycling whenever possible; for example, some of the wood came from old bowling alley lanes.

"We are still tweaking the building for better energy savings," says David Orr, the director of the Environmental Studies Program and the driving force in making this monument to environmental sanity a reality. "We know we can do better. As Wes Jackson [a geneticist carrying on advanced experiments in agricultural ecology at his Land Institute in Kansas] likes to say of his work, 'This is Kittyhawk, and we're just ten feet off the ground.'"

Actually, the center is flying much higher than that. Not only does it work as planned, but it has become what Orr and his associates intended: not just a place where classes are taught, but a teacher itself in stone and mortar. Orr refers to it as "crystallized pedagogy," a show-and-tell project on a grand, universal scale. And in the process of teaching invaluable ecological lessons to students, faculty, and local community simply by being what it is, the building has generated some five hundred news stories in everything from the *New York Times* to the *Chronicle of Higher Education*. "The collateral benefits of the publicity, funding, and increased enrollment are much greater than the $7.4 million total project cost, and these very tangible benefits continue to accrue," says Orr. "This is another example of how, when you do something right, there are advantages that the bean counters could never predict, including actual financial profits."

The historic moment came in January 2000, fittingly at the beginning of a new millennium. The valve on the sewer pipe to the city waste-treatment plant was turned off, and the biological in-house system, called a Living Machine, capable of handling twenty-three hundred gallons of wastewater per day, was turned on. Academia was acknowledging and teaching one of life's most important and fundamental truths: *when you flush the toilet, the shit doesn't disappear.*

The process of water purification is similar to that of Paws, Incorporated, but the configuration of the system is quite different. For one thing, the solar greenhouse that covers the wastewater treatment "facility"—it should be called a garden, not a facility—is right there *in* the building—not only in it, but very visible in it. You can hardly pass in and out of the center, or walk from office to classroom, without seeing it through big glass windows.

Before passing into the Living Machine garden, wastewater moves from the restrooms into an anaerobic digester, where solids and fats settle out and BOD (biological oxygen demand) is reduced by half. The wastewater then flows into closed aerobic tanks, where it is aerated by pumps and diffusers. (Remember, the electricity to run these oxygenators is being generated through the building's solar panels.) The water then flows into the Living Machine, where in large tanks full of thriving plants and animals like snails and goldfish, purification and clarification are completed. The last stage is unique. The floor of the Living Machine is an artificial wetland, three feet deep with gravel and small stones through which the water moves on a slight grade. Bacteria on the roots of plants growing in the gravel complete the denitrification process. Next the water flows through an ultraviolet disinfection unit to make sure no harmful pathogens remain and into a holding tank outside. The water then goes into a pressurized holding tank for reuse in the building's toilets.

What Jim Davis and David Orr have achieved indoors stands as an almost perfect model for what was taking place outdoors in wastewater treatment technology over the last decade or so. Outdoors, these biological wastewater-treatment systems have come to be called "constructed wetlands." They have been applied successfully to home septic systems, to small community wastewater-treatment facilities, and even to treating industrial wastes where conditions are favorable. In all cases, what starts out as biological filtration systems culminates in ponds, often called polishing ponds, where the water is clean enough to support food plants and animals. In other words, we are now looking at not only lower-cost and environmentally safe water treatment, but a transformation of dirty water into life-giving water.

Driving in southern Ohio one day many years ago, I passed over a creek and noticed that the water flowing in it was bright orange. I was so startled that I stopped and backed up to look again. Sure enough, a ribbon of bright orange was winding through green foliage. For some weird reason, I immediately thought of a dragon. And I knew the dragon's name was Pollution. I learned later that the orange creek was the result of acid leachate seeping out of abandoned coal mines in the raped hills of southern Ohio. The leachate wasn't always orange or reddish. It could be crystal clear, making creeks look like trout streams, but trout streams in which nothing, absolutely nothing, lived.

Sherwood Reed of the Army Corps of Engineers knew all about orange creek water. About the time that John Todd was starting to design biological wastewater-treatment systems like the one at Paws, Incorporated, Reed was going through a change in his thinking about waste management, too. Waste management was the field of experimentation in which he was involved at the time. As he told me later, when I was writing about orange creeks: "Like most engineers, I was trained in the 'black box' approach. To achieve any specified level of water quality was a matter of the proper sequence of chemical and mechanical operations—pressing the right buttons at the right time. The idea of using natural systems like a constructed wetland to purify water seemed crazy to me and I flat out said it wouldn't work." But the result of two decades (the seventies and eighties) of work that he and fellow scientists in the Corps of Engineers and elsewhere were doing, he had to change his mind. In this new frontier of water treatment, there were more unknowns than knowns, but it was now obvious to him that natural systems could clean dirty water and do it more cheaply than the black box approach.

One of the places where constructed wetland ponds turned out to be especially effective was in purifying acid mine leachate—the orange creek dragons. As Woody told me the story, an observant worker in the Bureau of Mines noticed a stand of cattails growing vigorously in the reddish leach water seeping out of an abandoned coal mine. He also noticed that when the water flowed out of the cattail stand, it was clearer. Hmmmmmm. A controlled experiment was set up—a constructed wetland similar to the one at the mine site.

Sure enough, exposing acid mine wastes to aerobic oxidizing conditions in a cattail wetland pond allowed much of the excess iron content to drop out.

Since then, hundreds of these artificial wetland ponds have been constructed to clean up wastewater. If the system would work on mine leachate, it would of course work much better on human waste, which decomposes much faster. Eventually, constructed wetland systems started replacing home septic systems in some rural areas and in small rural communities. In many instances, especially in Europe and Asia, quite large systems for towns and industrial plants have also proven practical. And after the water runs through primary and secondary stages of purification, fish can thrive in tertiary polishing ponds, along with cattails, bulrushes, duckweed, and other plants that have known value for protein food.

The cattail is a very remarkable plant. Every cattail will produce thousands of seeds, which fall into the water and sprout. (On my little pond I have to cut off the seed heads before they mature and throw them away, or else my pond would in a few years be totally engulfed with cattails.) Because of the cattail's vigor in spreading, wildlife advisors sometimes recommend burning off old stands of stalks. I have helped burn off acres of cattails in early spring in the swamps along the Minnesota River and have never seen any advantage to it except to improve the stand.

All parts of the plant are useful—a potential food source of more than dilettante interest. The root rhizomes are a very practical food, and the young stalk shoots, young seed heads, and pollen are also edible. (The long, tough summer leaves can be dried and used for chair canning and plaiting baskets.) I'm not wild about wild vegetables in general, but the cooked flesh of cattail rhizomes is tasty and filling. There are some stringy fibers toward the outside of the cooked rhizomes, but these can be easily separated as you eat.

The rhizomes can be used as a flour, too. Instead of cooking, cut them into sections about four inches long and dry them. They can be dried in the sun and air, or in a solar heater, or over a stove, or whatever. When they will snap in two rather crisply and the whitish powder falls out, they're dry enough. That powder is the flour you're after. It contains more protein than corn or rice and more fat and minerals than corn, rice, or wheat. Leland Marsh, who experimented years ago with cattails at the State University of New York at Oswego, observed that on land shaped and leveed so it could be flooded or drained at will, like a rice paddy, cattails could be a practical farm crop and livestock feed, if not human food. Cattails could produce thirty tons of flour per acre dry weight, he said, with enough rhizomes left in the soil to sprout the next year's crop. Thirty tons per acre is many times the amount that any crop of domesticated grain can yield. The highest wheat yield ever recorded is less than three tons per acre, and half that is considered a good crop.

On rhizomes dug up in the fall, you will find yellow-green shoots growing up to six inches long. These sprouts will make next year's plants. They will also make good eating right now, steamed like asparagus. These shoots are available all winter and early spring.

In the spring when the sprouts grow up out of the mud and water, they are still fairly tasty until about two feet tall and before the flowers appear. Eat them raw, boiled, or creamed. In May and June the flowers develop on the stalk, the female flower below the male. It is the female blossom that makes the fuzzy brown seed head from which cattail gets its name. When the male flower is just emerging from its (his?) sheath and beginning to turn from green to yellow, it can be cut off and cooked. Strip away the husk and boil as you would sweet corn. This is gourmet food in some fancy restaurants, but evidently I haven't got the hang of it yet, because "sweet corn" cattails I've tried to prepare were barely edible.

A little later, the male flower produces fine golden pollen, which can be used as a substitute for flour in pancake batter. Bend a flower over and shake it into a paper bag to collect the pollen. It's slow going, but about thirty heads should give you enough for a batch of pancakes. Mix batter as you would ordinarily.

There is always a rhizome connecting one plant to the next, so you should be able to locate some between the plants without any problem. I generally just reach down into the mud and feel around until I find one, pull it loose from the base of one plant, and then pull steady until it breaks loose altogether.

Because modern humans are so terribly fearful of even the remotest possibility of food contamination, eating plants (or fish) that have been reared in polishing ponds is going to be taboo in our society for a long time, except in places where people are hungry. Americans no longer understand hunger. It amazes me that every morning millions of people going to work risk death from the heavy metal of automobiles on the highways but fear even the tiniest parts per billion of so-called "heavy metals" in their food. They pretend to abhor the idea of spreading properly treated human waste (biosolids) on farmland because of an infinitesimal amount of "heavy metals" that might be involved. But a certain amount of almost all metals is necessary for healthy plant growth, and many soils are short of them. Vitamin tablets have "heavy metals" in them. The biosolids industry should start calling them "lite metals."

Here's a true story that might persuade the American consumer to lighten up a little on this matter. Growing along the railroad track south of Harpster, Ohio, when I was a kid was a stand of the biggest, juiciest elderberries ever to grace the earth. The reason the berries were so lush was that the bushes grew beside a little stream of sewage water running out of the village in an open ditch. This was of course years ago, before the EPA existed. We went out of our way to pick these elderberries, even though there were plenty of other stands closer to home, because they were so tasty. Mom made elderberry pies out of them. We discussed, and so did our parents, whether there was any danger involved in eating berries from bushes growing so close to human sewage. We decided that there was no difference between eating elderberries fertilized by human waste and eating corn fertilized by cow manure. Maybe we were wrong, but we were healthy. Half of China would have starved by now if the Chinese didn't use night soil to fertilize their gardens.

In 1989, while writing for *BioCycle,* a magazine covering waste recycling, I became acquainted with Viet Ngo, president of the Lemna Corporation in Minnesota. Ngo, whose name is pronounced "no" but, considering his positive attitude, ought to be pronounced "yes," came to America at the age of eighteen, in 1970, on a scholarship sponsored by the South Vietnamese government. As with most scholarships, the money was not nearly enough to support him while he acquired engineering degrees. He worked as a janitor in his spare time and kept his eyes open for opportunity.

Always drawn to nature, he was surprised to observe that duckweed, a floating water plant common in his native Vietnam, was also common in cold Minnesota, where it often covered ponds and small lakes like a green scum in summer. It was not often, in his experience, that one and the same plant would grow so well in two widely different climates. Duckweed, obviously, was very adaptive. It was also wonderful food for ducks. He stored that little bit of knowledge away in the computer of his brain for possible further use.

Out of school, he worked for several engineering firms and then started his own consulting business. "Consulting gets to be sort of dull after a while," he told me, "so I began thinking of business opportunities in the field of ecology, which always interested me. Minnesota, which means 'land of ten thousand lakes,' so I understand, was experiencing serious eutrophication problems in many of its lakes. I wondered if there were solutions that were environmentally safe."

He remembered duckweed, which he knew was a fast-growing, high-protein plant that could absorb lots of nitrogen and phosphorus as well as heavy metals. Research showed what he had suspected: duckweed grew just about everywhere in the world. Moreover, it could grow very fast indeed. "Would you believe that a single plant can double its weight in eighteen hours?" he said, amazement still sounding in his voice.

But that wasn't all. Duckweed contained twice the protein that alfalfa did and was so rich in amino acids that it was not grouped nutritionally with other plants but with meat, fish, and dairy products! It would surely be easier to process duckweed than most plants because there were no bulky stems to deal with. "What I was looking at," said Ngo, "was a food that could be very important to Third World countries. In fact, my inclination is usually to think of duckweed in terms of food rather than purifying water. Unlike the U.S., there are many countries where adequate food still takes priority over clean water."

But it was as a water purifier that Ngo found the first market for his revolutionary idea. In 1983 he started the Lemna Corporation (*Lemnaceae* is the Latin name for the duckweed family of plants) and began exploring ways to use duckweed to clean up wastewater. The first problem he confronted was that the faintest breeze had a tendency to blow the light scum to the edges of his ponds. Again, as he had approached the potential of duckweed itself, he found a solution in nature. He noticed that any object placed on the water and anchored so that it wouldn't drift arrested the movement of the duckweed too. Using plastic strips formed into a hexagonal grid, the geometric form that honeybees use to give strength to the fragile structure of honeycomb, Ngo built his grids, each hexagonal side ten feet long. Floated on the water and anchored in place, the grid held the duckweed over the entire water surface. Not only did the grid stop the duckweed from drifting, but the quiescent water that resulted enhanced duckweed's other important benefit: odor control. The combination of quiet water and the aerobic zone that the duckweed mat maintained over the anaerobic waste water stopped odors from rising into the air.

In 1985 Ngo patented his grid system, and he went on to develop a harvester, resembling an amphibious grain harvester, that skimmed off the duckweed. From the floating grid he hung porous baffle curtains down to near the pond bottom. Water flowing into the pond went into a sort of manifold of pipes down in the water and then flowed out evenly through ports in the manifold. The baffles suspended from the floating barriers acted as a flow control system so that the water moved evenly and ever so slowly through the pond. Sensors monitored the system's performance and controlled feed stations automatically metered out precise quantities of nutrients and micronutrients as needed to optimize treatment. After the pond was ready, each hexagonal cell of the floating barrier was seeded with duckweed. Complete coverage took place in from one to four weeks, depending on the weather and the nutrient content of the water.

One of Ngo's first clients was Del Monte, which was processing peas and sweet corn at Sleepy Eye, Minnesota (whose townspeople are nothing like what that name implies). The town's wastewater treatment system was having trouble purifying the effluent from the plant to acceptable limits before discharging into a nearby creek. Ngo installed a Lemna system in a polishing pond in 1986. The duckweed eliminated odor and algae problems and cleaned the effluent water enough to meet discharge requirements.

"And we could do that at half to a third of the cost of a mechanical system," Ngo said at the time. "Operation cost was low too, because the energy used is from the sun."

Since those pioneer days, the Lemna Corporation, as Lemna International, has gone on to glory, successfully addressing all kinds of environmental problems throughout the world. You can check out its progress on its Web site on the Internet.

Ponds are beginning to be used as efficient collectors of solar heat for many purposes, especially to heat and cool buildings. Many homeowners have already installed geothermal heating and air conditioning systems that use heat pumps to draw on the earth's steady temperature of about fifty-five degrees Fahrenheit for warming their houses in winter and cooling them in summer at low cost. A few have opted to use backyard ponds the same way, since water in the bottom of the pond remains at a stable earth temperature, too. Using a pond for geothermal heating and cooling is generally more expensive than using the earth itself, but for the person planning on a backyard pond anyway, this would be a way to justify some of its cost. Electric utility companies are energetically pushing geothermal. They will be glad to discuss the pros and cons of ponds for this purpose and will even show you houses where ponds are being used this way.

It is easy to get carried away with all the possibilities. Imagine a pond, just off the back porch, that provides reliable and efficient heat, air conditioning, fresh fish, swimming, ice skating, a spectacular piece of landscaping to look at, and a source of artistic inspiration that Monet would find worthy of his canvas. All wonderful things start off as someone's crazy dream.

STRINGS OF PEARLY POOLS

How many creeks did you drive by or cross over this morning on your way to work? Unless you are a pond lover, I bet that you will not know—and not think that you have any reason to know. Creeks are invisible to most people.

This unconscious ignorance is most unfortunate. Our survival depends on water, and on our constant awareness of where the water, moving by gravity over the face of the earth, is coming from and where it is going. One practical example: if you buy a property that has a tiny rivulet at the edge of your backyard, be sure the house stands on suitably high ground above the rivulet. Otherwise, after heavy rains you might find a raging little river in your yard, filling your basement with water. I speak from experience. Our backyard gives no indication at all that the runoff from about thirty acres flows through it. We had to build up the first-floor doorsill a foot to keep water out of the house. Only once in thirty years was the high sill necessary, but one flooded basement every thirty years is one too many.

Water is the blood of the soil, and creeks are the primary veins that carry away the excess to the rivers, which carry it to the seas.

Ponds hold back some of the water and so decrease a little the effects of floods. Creeks, by their natural tendency to meander, also lower the risk of flooding. You can tell which farmers are water-illiterate, because they straighten creeks in the hope of gaining a little more ground to grow surplus corn on. Straightening creeks increases the threat of flooding downstream. Cities show their water illiteracy by erecting floodwalls, which also increase the threat of flooding downstream. But society does not care. Protect my property, people demand. Flood out the poor unfortunates downstream who can't afford flood walls. Eventually the result is New Orleans, through which the Mississippi runs between levees *higher* than the level of part of the city. To keep the city from being inundated, uncounted dollars have been spent not only to build levees but to divert part of the Mississippi's waters into another river above the city. Some hydrologists believe it is only a matter of time before a flood will come along that will override the levees and devastate the city.

Children and farmers treasure creeks, the first as a source of play and the second as a source for livestock water and as a place to run field tile drains into. Much of the most productive soil in the Corn Belt would be untillable were it not for tile drainage, and most of the tile drainage would be prohibitively expensive were it not for creeks to act as outlets for the tile. Where there is not enough fall to the land to form creeks, farmers dig enormously expensive drainage ditches, which, by hastening the exit of surplus water from their land, also contribute to flooding.

Real-estate advertisements in rural areas are fond of the phrase "ever-running" or "year-round" stream, by which they mean a small creek fed by enough springs so that it doesn't dry up in the summer. A shepherd or stockman, seeking pastureland, puts a high value on an ever-running stream, because it means a constant source of water for his animals without any expense. The old maps in homesteading days marked the good springs as assiduously as today's maps mark highways, because reliable springs were important to the pioneer economy. Most of the important springs of yesteryear in our county have gone dry because of the advance of "civilization" by way of intensive grain farming or urban sprawl. If someday there is a major shift from grain farming to grass farming and pond farming, as seems to be beginning to happen, the springs will be renewed and the creeks will again become "ever-running."

Our creek, or "crick" as we persist in saying, is still spring fed, still ever-running. The springs that feed it bubble up from the bed of the stream, whereas in former times large springs fed into it from flanking hillsides. How long the streambed springs will continue to flow I do not know. They exist for only about a mile upstream from our place. Above that the creek dries up in dry summers. An old resident of the county who once lived in the house next to us, and to whom I spoke about these matters in 1975, when he was around ninety years old, said that in his boyhood, when the big springs yet lived, our creek ran hip deep in the pools between the riffles, and the pools were full of fish two to three pounds in size. The creek now scarcely maintains two feet of water in the deepest pools and rarely supports fish weighing more than a quarter of a pound.

By running year round, our creek provides not just reliable stock water but an amazing variety of aquatic life: waterfowl like ducks, herons, and kingfishers; mammals like muskrat, mink, raccoons, and opossums; and, although fewer in number and size than previously, fish, frogs, snakes, turtles, crayfish, and even mussels. During droughts, when other creeks dry up, ours becomes something akin to a farm pond, although skinny and long rather than oval, drawing all native wild mammals and birds to it.

Learning the species of fish in a creek can be a most absorbing hobby. All you need is a seine. Walk upstream through the deeper pools, holding ahead of you the seine stretched wide across the whole width of the creek and with its bottom dragging on the creek bed. Prod the ends of the seine handles under the banks of the creek, where the fish will try to hide as you approach. When you come to a riffle, lift the seine and examine what you have caught. Likely as not, you will be surprised. I have seined our creek for fifty years so far, and although the variety is not nearly as great as it once was, I still can catch several kinds of the smaller minnows—bluntnose, fathead, blacknose dace, plus the white sucker, the creek chub, and an occasional chain pickerel. Years ago, we regularly caught various sunfish, black bullheads, and yellow bullheads also.

I remember from my childhood the first years when the creek above the part that is spring-fed went dry in summer. I would rescue dying fish from the deeper pools, which were last to dry up, and I distinctly remember all the species named above. I'd put the fish in a bucket of water and transfer them to our horse trough at the barn. Even at that early age, I was very troubled by the dying fish but did not know, nor did anyone else, that they were dying because humans were continuing to cut down forests, continuing to install more and more tile drainage, and continuing to farm more intensively. In springtime, with plenty of water in the creek, fish from Tymochtee Creek, a small river into which our creek runs, came upstream to recharge the fish population in the creek; but little by little the days when we could catch a string of bullheads and sunfish passed. Today my grandsons and I catch chubs barely big enough to hook.

Once, fifteen years ago, about a dozen northern pike came up the creek in spring and became trapped in our spring-fed section when the water level went down again. As far as we can reason, they came from the large reservoir in the Killdeer Plains Wildlife Refuge, upstream from us. Occasionally water is let out of the reservoir into the Tymochtee, and the fish escaped that way and then swam up our creek. In any event, they grew to be about a foot long, monsters for our creek. My son caught a couple of them. It was no easy feat. We had to *crawl* up to the section of creek where the pike were trapped. If the fish saw us they would spook. From a prone position my son would cast a daredevil lure into the creek and then proceed to reel it in. Remember, we're talking here about less than two feet of water and a creek width of maybe six feet. We knew when a pike was going to strike the lure because we could easily see its wake as it shot toward the lure. I took pictures of the pike my son caught. No one would otherwise believe a fish that large could survive in so small a body of water. At the next high water, the pike disappeared. They probably ended up in Lake Erie.

A creek seems at a cursory glance to be nothing but a ditch with water of a more or less uniform depth in it. That is never the case, unless the creek has been artificially straightened in the last half-century or so. A gentle warm-water creek is actually a series of little garden pools connected by shallow trickles—I like to say a string of pool pearls with links of silver riffles. A creek assumes this pool-riffle-pool form from the motion of water going downstream. Water, like a habitual criminal, never goes straight for very long. When it hits an obstruction along a bank, however slight, it will bounce toward the other bank. When it hits that bank, it tends to bounce back again. If the water hits an obstruction in the middle of the creek or on the bed of the creek, a similar bouncing effect occurs. What looks to the eye like a uniform current following gravity downstream is actually many little individual eddies chaotically caroming against one another as the water makes its fitful way downstream. You can easily observe this action by throwing twigs in the water and watching them float downstream. Two twigs started side by side will invariably take quite different courses.

This meandering, agitated motion also means that the water is constantly speeding up and slowing down, as your twigs will show you too. When it speeds up, water tends to dig up silt and carry it along. When the current slows, water tends to drop its load of silt. Thus pools and shallows are formed, as well as curves in the creek banks. The result is another example of the delightful variety that nature constantly produces in direct contradiction to the heavy hand of uniformity that human commerce seems to demand of it. Generally, the outside curves of a meander carve steep banks, and the inside curves, miniature beaches. If the meandering action of a stream could be speeded up so that every second represented a century, the stream would be seen to wriggle sinuously like a snake. Eventually a meander curves around so pronouncedly that it cuts itself off from the mainstream and becomes an oxbow pond. In all these natural actions of current moving by gravity, the creek, or river, forms habitat for many more kinds of plants and animals than a straight, man-made ditch will. The meandering, as already mentioned, also slows down the rush of water in heavy rain or spring thaws to lessen the effects of flooding downstream.

In mountain streams different conditions prevail. The fall downhill is much steeper consistently over longer stretches, so the current attains a much greater velocity than our mud-bottomed, flat-country streams. Mountain streams in hilly areas are almost entirely rock, the soil either having been washed away long ago or perhaps having never existed there at all. But the current, however more rapid, usually maintains the same stairstepped alternation between rapids and pools, though the alternations are farther apart and more pronounced.

On our creek, like many others, humans have not appreciated the natural, meandering journey of water seeking its own level and have speeded up the process of cutting off meanders with straight runs of ditch. Two miles upstream from our farm, at what I call Old Home (where I grew up), my father straightened our creek by cutting a new channel through the neck of a forming oxbow. He feared the outer curve of the meander was going to cut into one of his cultivated fields. The creek would have cut through the meander by itself eventually and stopped that threat, but Dad did not have a century to wait. I suspect the cost of cutting a new channel for the creek about equaled the loss his cornfield would have suffered, but humans can't think in a framework that extends beyond two or three generations. Nor are they inclined to think beyond the borders of their own property. What difference did it make if a little bit of flooding water rushed downstream a little bit faster than it would have if the meander were in place? We did not understand how billions of "little bits" add up to something not so little.

Closer to our place, my great-uncles straightened the creek again, although there seemed to be no pressing need to do so, other than that my Germanic ancestors loved straight lines. They associated curves with poor farming and temptations to socialism and sex, the two great threats to what they considered the well-being of society even though they were immersed in both of them. They accepted government subsidies whenever it was convenient to do so, which was always whether they needed the money or not. And nothing in family history would lead one to conclude that they were pure of heart and soul in matters of sex. My grandfather drained a large man-made farm pond on the back of Old Home for the stated purpose of acquiring more cropland. But just a few years ago, I learned from an elderly gentleman of the neighborhood that this farm pond was the center of some shocking "high-liggety" in the good old days. The farm youth of the late 1800s, so canonized as innocents by the traditional literature of the time, used this isolated pond for nude swimming. Both sexes. Then they would go horseback riding, still nude, sometimes two on the same horse.

In both cases of creek straightening described above, nature was not hurt except perhaps by more flooding downstream, because the land cut off in the oxbows became in one case a wetland and in the other case woodland. But thousands of old oxbows have been turned into cornfields, often at no profit because of routine flooding.

Children who grow up beside a clean, small creek (by small I mean not deep enough to pose the danger of drowning) are very fortunate. I don't know how many hours of play I whiled away along our creek as a youngster, wading, swimming, fishing, trapping, ice skating, racing toy boats, camping, finding arrowheads and pretty rocks, building toy waterwheels, fashioning clay pots and mud pies, building little dams and bridges. I'm sure it would amount to a good quarter of my childhood. If you add up the cost of modern toys that would not be needed where children have creeks to play in, a stretch of stream through a backyard is probably worth nearly half the cost of the lot.

Actually I never quit playing in our creek. I'm still at it, now accompanied by grandchildren. A game that never fails to please children is racing toy boats or sticks in the current. Another favorite is trying to cross the creek without getting a shoe full of water. The time-honored way to do this is to select a steep bank, where the water is busy cutting a meander, and jump from it, usually a height of about five feet on our creek, to the much lower "beach" across from it. With a running start, a child can leap a stream several feet wide, and the flight is giddy enough to lure even old men. Old men, however, are apt to land in the water if not in the doctor's office.

Not only is racing toy boats or sticks an excellent way to study how the current works in a creek; the chaos of currents also makes the boat racing fun. No one knows, at the start of a race over, say, a hundred-yard stretch of creek, whose "boat" is going to win. No one can even predict if any of the boats will make it the whole way to the assigned finish line without lodging on the shoreline.

Some people use the knowledge of how water moves in a current to "develop" a creek, especially a trout stream, for better fishing. They build wooden or stone structures in their streams to preserve banks, to provide hiding places for trout, to concentrate stream flow and therefore increase velocity through a particular section, to aerate the water, and to force the water to dig out deeper pools between riffles. I think these devices are rarely necessary but are another delightful way to play in the creek like a child without appearing to be doing so. If you decide to develop your creek, be sure not to obstruct it in a way that would stop fish from moving upstream.

Generally speaking, it is illegal to dam any navigable stream, but it's okay to put in a little stone structure across a wading creek. Children will spend hours at the task. If the dam is no more than a foot high, fish will leap right up over it. All kinds of fish, even little fish, will jump the dam. One day as we sat on the bridge we had built across our creek right above a little waterfall dam we had thrown up with rocks, we were startled to see fish leap right up between our dangling legs and across the dam. Fish of five inches in length could leap triple their length! Bigger fish, like quarter-pound carp, could clear the dam easily. Some fish, instead of jumping, would swim *vertically* up the foot-high column of water pouring over the dam.

But it was the jumping fish that intrigued me most. How did they know how far to jump? If the dam had been higher, could they have jumped higher? If lower, would they have put less energy into their leap? Why had they decided to jump at all, when other fish were demonstrating that they could swim over? Had the fish checked out the whole length of the dam before deciding that there was no way through it but only over it, or had they jumped out of impulse or instinct upon first meeting the obstacle? Had they perhaps jumped for the sheer joy of jumping?

A few days later the marvelous cleverness I thought the fish had demonstrated was replaced with what to a human seemed extreme stupidity. The same minnows that had muscled their way over the dam were now, after the water level had fallen to normal, allowing the slow current to carry them into crevices between the rocks of the dam. There they became trapped and would have died if we hadn't rescued them. They had not the wit to swim away from the dam before they became entrapped. To alleviate the problem, I shoveled dirt and gravel up against the rocks so that the fish could not drift into them.

It is probably a good idea to open at least the middle of even a little dam after a day of play, anyway. If you leave the dam blocking the current all the way across the creek, water flowing downstream slows as it hits the dam and drops its silt. Eventually the upstream bed fills to the height of the dam, making a fairly extended section of the creek shallower and wider than desirable. But to balance that, the water will have dug a deeper hole below the dam.

Trout will not survive in our warm-water creek. Trout need water fifty to sixty degrees Fahrenheit, shady banks to keep it that way, and occasional rapids or riffles to aerate the water. But warm-water fish benefit from shade too, and all creek banks ought to have some trees on them. Tree roots at the water's edge offer hiding places or shelter for fish and other aquatic life, and slow down bank erosion.

Creeks have always been a vital part of my life, wherever I wandered. When I lived in Minnesota, I had daily access to a wondrous marsh network of spring-fed trout streams. We dined on watercress all winter, even in times of zero temperatures, because the spring water didn't freeze. We also had a steady supply of rainbow trout. There was nothing quite so surprising as catching a three-quarter-pound rainbow lurking along the grassed-over bank edge of a stream that was only two feet wide.

I loved the clear springs running out of this marsh into the Minnesota River. I became a marsh rat, haunting the inner recesses of the swamp where hardly any other human ventured. When the Minnesota River was running full at near-flood stage, the water backed up into the steep-banked mouths of these creeks. There would be a place upstream in the creeks where the muddy wall of floodwater stopped and the clear spring water, dammed up, so to speak, by the floodwater, began. The two waters would be as clearly delineated from each other as if there were a sheet of glass between them. It was a weird but wonderful sight. Fish, mostly carp, would swim out of the muddy water and become spookily visible in the clear water, a situation that they were evidently not aware of. Sometimes we would try to spear them as they appeared. Once, on impulse, I took off my clothes and swam to the junction between muddy and clear water. I could watch my hand all but disappear into the cloud of muddy floodwater. Suddenly a huge carp swam up, perhaps wondering what

I might be, and then disappeared back into the dark water. I was so fascinated I almost forgot that I had to surface and get some air.

It suddenly strikes me, as I contemplate that Minnesota day, that I have lived with my feet, and often my whole body, in creeks, rivers, and ponds all over the Midwest. I must have fish genes in me. I keep looking for fins to develop. My earliest memory is of playing in a creek with my parents. They would drive the car right down into a rocky stream near where we lived, in Newark, Ohio, and wash it while they splashed as childishly as my sister and I did.

In southern Indiana, in seminary boarding school, my friends and I spent every second of time allowed (and some that was not allowed) in the woods and along a creek that sported the most beautiful little fish I have ever seen, a red, silver, and blue minnow not as big as a finger. I never got over the fascination of catching a few of them (using a shirt for a seine) and just staring at their unbelievable tropical coloring. I later learned that they were called rainbow darters (*Etheostoma caeruleum*), but we called them American minnows because they were red, white, and blue.

It was on this creek that my friends and I developed a use for moving water that I have not seen discussed anywhere. One of our teachers, a Father Sylvester, was a farmer at heart (he taught Latin with a look of sheer agonized boredom on his face), but in his spare time he grew several acres of melons and also tended the apple orchard. I admired him greatly, mostly because he could tell jokes better than anyone I knew, but also because at the height of his "career" as a farmer he was involved in a serious automobile accident. He had to wear a huge cast on his neck, which would have incapacitated almost anyone. But he kept right on tending his big watermelon patch. Have you ever tried to hoe with a cast on your neck? Because of his condition, he occasionally relied on students to help him. But he was a realist. He knew our help would come at a price because, as he had learned in previous years, some of us were master melon thieves. At harvest time he suddenly developed a distinct lack of interest in any more help from us and stationed himself in the middle of the patch, where he could keep an eye on things. The watermelon patch lay right next to the creek. We took stock of the situation. We approached the watermelons by crawling along the creek bank out of his sight, snaked up to the edge of the patch on our bellies, rolled melons back to the bank and into the water, and backed off ourselves, still out of sight, until we were back at the entrance to the field. Then we stood up, brushed the dirt from our clothes, and sauntered innocently through the patch asking if there was work we could help with. No, no, he said graciously. He appreciated all we'd done for him but picking ripe watermelons was a skill that students were not especially endowed with, he explained. Then he followed us all the way through the patch and beyond to make sure we did not carry a few melons out with us. In the woods beyond the patch, we waited patiently until our melons floated down to us. As I think back on that incident, I will bet a load of watermelons that Father Sylvester knew exactly what we were doing.

In Pennsylvania, on the Wissahicon Creek, I learned that ice skating downstream was much easier and faster than ice skating upstream.

In Michigan, on the Grand River, I learned that a hooked ten-pound carp can pull a rowboat and two fishermen upstream. I also learned not to walk on thin ice ever, ever again. I almost drowned when I went through the ice. My friend Herm pulled me out with a long branch just before all the ice around me gave way. The river was in thaw time, and the water was deep and very swift. Herm saved my life. A strange thing: I had not seen or talked to him for twenty-five years, and a few days after I wrote down this incident, he called me from halfway across the country.

In Kentucky the creek through the farm where my wife grew up, and along the banks of which we spent many a pleasant Sunday in our courting days, has disappeared. I mean literally. It was such a pretty creek, rock-bottomed and singing all the way, a great place for wading children, as Carol and her brothers and sisters often used it in earlier days. But the Metropolitan Water District ran a sewer line through the hollow, and the creek went down a hole and never came back up. We all stood in the hollow not quite believing what had happened. After running millions of years, overnight the creek was gone, and all its fish and aquatic life with it. And all the civilized promises to restore the hollow back to the way it had been disappeared too.

This is just one of many reasons why I seek the brotherhood of wild nature. There is a bond among writers never to say it, but the truth is that the natural world—the real world—would survive much better without humans.

If you don't have a creek to enjoy, you can make one—at least a little one—about as easily as you can make a pond. Seep springs can sometimes be cleaned out and rocked up into a pool. The overflow can be made to trickle into a tiny creek or a series of tiny pools and riffles.

What most people do, however, is to make an entirely artificial creek. A concealed pump moves water from a filled pool at the end of the "creek" to the pool at its beginning. It is not necessary to "run" the creek constantly but only when you are there to enjoy the rippling water. A friend of mine who made a tumbling creek in his garden came to regret it, because he could not keep neighborhood children from playing in it and injuring rare garden plants close by. If you have children, that incident perhaps tells you the real reason you should make a creek in your backyard: for your children's amusement.

How you build a little stream will depend entirely on the amount of space you have and the lay of the land. The steeper the grade, the more pearly pools you will need to install, and the more rapid the riffles between the pools. On land quite steep, you end up with a series of pools with tiny waterfalls connecting them. If you go to garden shows, or visit a garden pool dealer, you will find more ideas on how to do this than you could ever put into practice. The high pool at the beginning of your creek and the low pool at the end of it can be big enough to hold fish permanently or at least most of the year. You can choose from hundreds of kinds of colorful garden-pool fish, like koi or goldfish (members of the carp family), or you can stock various colorful sunfish, like bluegills, pumpkinseeds, longear sunfish, redear sunfish, green sunfish, and perch, and have a good meal occasionally. It is beyond me that garden pool lovers stick with the brightly colored koi and goldfish when good-tasting, nearly as colorful native fish are available. I guess I think too much with my stomach.

Most artificial creeks are hardly more than a hundred feet long, but if you have room and a gentle slope that does not draw much runoff water to it, you can make one quite long. I have seen artificial creeks as long as a football field. Walking beside them, you'd never dream they were fake. Probably it is best in this situation, especially if the soil is sandy or gravelly, to lay down heavy plastic or rubber liner in the creek bed, so as not to lose water, and cover the liner with pebbles.

Another enchanting idea is to make a little creek that runs into your farm pond and use it to aerate the pond. When you dig the pond, pile the dirt from the excavation into a mound close by. Then dig a well on top of the mound and put a windmill on it. Then build a little gurgling creek from the pump spout down to the pond. When the wind blows, the water flows and gurgles oxygen into the pond. This is a rather expensive way to build a creek. Even if you can get a used windmill from Amish crews who specialize in moving wind-mills, you are still talking at least a thousand dollars. A new windmill costs around three thousand, and the well digging of course is an-other expense. But the windmill and pump also keep the pond full and can be used as a source of water for livestock, and a source of your own drinking water, if and when the electric blackouts reach your part of the country. The pump and creek can also relieve you of the cost of an aerator, if you think your pond needs one.

Incidentally, pond water, and no doubt some exclusively spring-fed streams, can be rendered safe to drink with proper filtering and disinfecting. Local health authorities, extension service personnel, and manufacturers of filtering and chlorinating devices are all at your service. *Private Water Systems,* a publication written years ago by U.S. Department of Agriculture extension engineers, is particularly pertinent. I'm sure extension engineers elsewhere have similar helpful publications. I am not going to go into detail on filtering and disinfecting water, because you will need to consult local health codes anyway.

The best reason to build a creek remains: it's a great "toy" to give children if they don't have a real creek. Kids can play in it, unlike a pond, without fear of drowning. They can splash and wade and get muddy, and who cares. Childhood lasts such a short time in these mad days of the twenty-first century.

SHAMBAUGH POND

When I helped survey and plan the Shambaugh Pond, I could not have predicted, by the wildest stretch of imagination, how it would become an intimate part of my life forty years later. I was working for the Soil Conservation Service back then. One of the services SCS rendered was surveying and designing ponds for land-owners. Dale Shambaugh owned a seventy-acre farm, in the middle of which, far back off the road, was a narrow, moderately steep-banked ravine ideally shaped for a pond of over half an acre with an embankment dam. Shambaugh was willing to spend the money to "do it right," he said, which pleased my boss and good friend, Don Hall, immensely. Don (now deceased) was accustomed to con-tending with landowners who could not understand why putting several hundred dollars more than the bare minimum into pond construction would pay off over the years. This would be especially true of Shambaugh Pond because it had a relatively large watershed and would require a fairly sophisticated dam. Don designed for him a pond that wouldn't leak, with an overflow outlet and emergency spillway capacity to withstand the worst flooding recorded in our county.

First we surveyed and made a contour map of the fields above the proposed pond site. That told us exactly how many acres sloped into the ravine. The number, twenty-five, was considerable for a pond of the size we planned to build, three-quarters of an acre, but not too many for a properly designed dam and spillway to handle. Once we knew the maximum amount of water that would be running into the pond using ten-year storm frequency records, we designed the pond outlets to handle that much water without overflowing the dam. We had to be certain on this point, because once high water starts flowing over an earthen dam, as I have said repeatedly, it can literally wash the middle of the embankment away in a matter of hours, sometimes in a matter of minutes.

Because we "did it right," the emergency spillway around the side of the dam seemed to be unnecessarily wide and gently graded, and Shambaugh grumbled a little at the added time (and therefore cost) this required of the bulldozer. But once sodded over, the spillway has stood the test of nearly a half-century of storms. The concrete drop outlet (mechanical spillway on the design plan) had to be quite large too, about one and a half feet by three feet, and covered with an iron grill so that floating debris or fish could not get into the pipe. The concrete box was about three feet deep with an eight-inch vitrified, self-sealing tile pipe running from it on down about fifteen feet and through the dam. The rather large size of the drain was related directly to the size of the watershed involved, the proper measurements set down in scs design manuals we used to guide us. The pipe had a concrete antiseep collar where it passed through the center of the dam. Because we took great pains to make a good, solid clay core down the center of the dam, there has been no significant leakage around the outlet pipe, as sometimes happens.

The slope of the dam on the outside is two to one, and on the inside three to one, the standard prescribed for the kind of clay we were working with. A sandy or siltier mix of dirt would have required a three-to-one or even four-to-one outer slope. Again these specifications are all written down in the design books for farm ponds and are still available from SCS offices.

The pond was designed to be eight and a half feet deep at the deepest place, with a six-foot average depth. The dirt for the dam was taken from the upper (shallower) end of the pond to gain the six-foot depth at that end. We designed a three-to-one slope for the shoreline, fairly steep, so as to discourage waterweeds around the edge of the pond.

After forty-some years, the shorelines and the upper end of the pond have grown shallower because of subsidence and soil carried in from erosion on the watershed. The pond's only weak point, in fact, is that the watershed land is regularly farmed, and after forty years enough soil has washed in to decrease the water depth at the upper end considerably. In spring the pond is muddy because of this, but by fall it is crystal clear again. There is no rip-rap around the pond, which is part of the reason that the bank has subsided and the shoreline is shallower than it was in earlier years. As a result, algae and waterweeds clog the edgewater. The muskrats, frogs, and fish love it, but it makes fishing difficult and swimming not possible unless you jump in the water off the pier that sticks out beyond the algae-infested shore.

This winter the algae caused a problem that I doubt anyone could have predicted. When thaw and rains brought a heavy flow of water into the pond, some of the dead shoreline algae from the preceding summer were pushed and pulled down against the dam and, inevitably, matted over the iron-grated outlet and plugged it. The water rose fast and began to flow out of the emergency spillway. Working feverishly, the owners finally got the grate unplugged. The water ripped and sucked and tore its way down the pipe with an enormous and frightening power. I wonder if a human, caught on that grate, might have been sucked through it, one body piece at a time. Fifteen feet below, the water shot full bore out of the eight-inch pipe. In only a few minutes the whole ravine below the dam was covered with water. The power of water with a fifteen-foot head is an awesome, frightening sight and sound. I was glad again that I had settled for only a very small pond in my pasture.

Obviously the algae must go. A combination of deepening shorelines, using herbicides, and introducing algae eaters like grass carp and sunfish ought to do it.

But that is really the least part of my involvement with Shambaugh Pond. Dale Shambaugh had a dream. He was one of that large number of people who, after tasting life in cities and finding it not to their liking, come home again, Thomas Wolfe to the contrary. His dream was to be a farmer. He worked for a local feed company and for established farmers for a while to learn about farming. He also got into the insurance business, at which he became quite successful. On weekends he and his wife would retreat to their sanctuary to live as farmers, tending their sheep, planning for the day when they could farm full time and sell insurance on the side. But one day when Dale climbed into the car and spoke to his wife, she did not reply. He spoke again; again, no reply. She had, without warning, suffered a stroke and would remain an invalid for the rest of her life. The time Dale had hoped to spend farming he spent caring for her. The pond that was the center of his life, and the train caboose he installed beside it as a cabin, he sold to his nephew and his wife, Jim and Diane Grafmiller.

Eventually the Grafmillers gave the seven acres and pond to their three children, one of whom is our daughter-in-law, Jill. When Dale died and his farm had to be sold, Jill and my son, Jerry, bought part of it, and Jill's brother David and his wife, Jodi, bought the other part.

Today these two couples are working hard to establish homesteads on their properties, and their children, two of them my grandsons, romp and play in a lifestyle strikingly similar to my own childhood. Dale Shambaugh, in attempting to come home again, made it possible for another generation to come back to the land.

Jerry and David fenced in the seven acres around the pond and planted alfalfa there. Carol and I gave them six yearling ewes to get them started in homesteading. The family gatherings and hockey games that had dwindled on the old home pond moved to Shambaugh Pond. Jerry and David are clearing brush and building barns, a chicken coop, and more fences to establish the self-reliant lifestyle that I had often thought I was writing about in vain.

So much of what these young people are doing is reminiscent of the "good old days" when people worked together in common interest to produce their own food, clothing, shelter, and recreation. Jerry and David, both rather quiet, work together easily, their partnership of physical effort adding up to a good deal more than just a simple mathematical doubling of labor, especially when wives and grandparents join in. For example, where one of them alone could put up a rod of fence in a day, two of them working together can put up three or more rods a day. Likewise, sharing the expense of tools that must be purchased makes the establishment of two homesteads somewhat less expensive than if two families established two homesteads independently. Carol and I share our tractors and machinery with them, spreading the cost over three families instead of one. Many of the costs of raising sheep we can share too. We can look after one another's place when someone has to be away. We cut wood together. As I grow older and need more help, I don't even have to ask. Since both Jerry and David know how to build, and in fact that's what Jerry does for a living, they will be able to use much of their own labor to build their homes. David's other career is in computers, a good skill to combine with homesteading, because some of the work he can do at home. Recently he put together parts from used computers to make one for Carol and me that cost us only a hundred dollars.

Although Shambaugh Pond is only three miles from our farm, the flora and fauna of the surrounding tree groves are, curiously, quite different from ours. Why this is true I can't say, but journeying from here to there is a bit like journeying botanically into another country. (Our grandsons call the new farm at Shambaugh Pond the "other country" to differentiate it from the homestead where Pawpaw and Grandmother live.) Three plant species not found here, in fact rarely found in this county, grow around Shambaugh Pond. One is chinquapin oak, whose acorns are not only edible but quite tasty. The oldest of these oaks is enormous in size. North central Ohio is not real chinquapin oak country, but nobody told the trees, I guess. Another somewhat rare species for this area, but more common farther south, is wahoo, a bush with pretty, bright pink flowers that can make an attractive ornamental. A third is bladdernut, which I have seen in Kentucky but never before in northern Ohio.

There are probably chinquapin oaks and wahoo and bladdernut in many other nearby locales, but I don't focus attention on these places nearly as sharply as I do on Shambaugh Pond and on our own acreage. I have a hunch this is why environmentalists put some plants on the endangered list too soon. In 2000 state botanists informed the public that several plants that they had hitherto concluded did not grow in Ohio anymore were "rediscovered." I'm sure they just hadn't looked closely enough before. I've read wildflower accounts that referred to trilliums as endangered. It's all right with me if officials want to list the white trillium as endangered, because doing so might persuade some people to protect it, but around here trillium is about as endangered as poison ivy.

The never-cultivated ravines around Shambaugh Pond also sport a rather dizzying variety of wildflowers, more species than we find on our place. I believe so many different flowers are present because Dale Shambaugh kept sheep, which cleared the woodland of brush for several years, encouraging wildflower growth. As soon as the sheep no longer pastured there, the wildflowers reappeared, as they have elsewhere, and will continue unless or until the woodland thickens with new tree seedlings and shades out the flowers. The other possibility is that the Shambaughs introduced more varieties but left no record of it. In one little hollow, in an area of not more than

150 feet in diameter, I counted more than twenty different kinds of wildflowers last spring.

Partly because of the pond's presence and partly because the area is rather remote from farmhouses, we have seen bald eagles regularly. Bald eagles, given the opportunity, will feast on fish. They may catch fish in the creek into which the pond outlet empties, as my son learned in a rather novel way. To get to the pond, one must drive through the creek, a rather exciting experience until it becomes routine. The creek exits into Tymochtee Creek, as our creek does. During spring floods rather large fish swim up this creek. We know that now because twice last spring, when Jerry went charging through the creek with his pickup, he came out on the other side with a fish flapping on the truck bumper. I don't think the eagles were nearly as surprised as he was.

Last summer, there was a large fish kill in the pond because of rapid turnover of the bottom and surface water. That may have drawn the eagles also. Many bass and even the huge old catfish that lived in the pond died. But although this situation seemed tragic at the time, it was actually a blessing, because there were too many bass in the pond anyway. Perhaps oxygen shortfall is nature's way of solving fish overpopulation problems. That there are no bluegills in the pond for the bass to feed on may be another reason that the bass are all stunted in size. But what I think happened was that fishermen over the years caught and removed all the big bass continually, leaving not enough to prey effectively on their own fry, as largemouth bass will do. The number, but not the size, of the bass grew exponentially. Now, after the die-off, the bass remaining will have a chance to grow to larger size and go on reproducing. We know there are quite a few bass remaining, because we have had no trouble catching a bunch for a fish fry.

Over the years the caboose that Shambaugh brought to the pond began to deteriorate, and on a recent weekend the whole family pitched in, repainted it, jacked up the floor, and resealed the roof. I got out of the work by taking our two grandsons on canoe rides on the pond, when they were not playing in the nearby creek with Grandmother. Their Grafmiller grandparents were painting, as were Jill and Jodi. Even Great-Grandma and -Grandpa Miller stopped by.

There are sometimes whole weekends when we all gather at Shambaugh Pond in the mutual interest of forging the homestead life for yet another generation. To watch two little grandsons, armed with hammers they can barely lift, pounding away at nails they are driving into hay mow floorboards of the new barn, makes me understand that all is right in the world. Hens will cackle here, lambs bounce, cows bellow, the hockey wars revive, children laugh and play. The good life has been passed on, and when I can't participate any longer, I shall rest in peace.

APPENDIX

Recommended Garden Suppliers

Lilypons Water Gardens, P.O. Box 10, Buckeystown, Md., 21717
Paradise Water Gardens, 14 May Street, Whitman, Mass., 02382

Recommended Publications

BioCycle magazine, J. G. Press, 419 State Avenue, Emmaus, Pa., 18049
Farm Pond Harvest, 1390 North, 14500 East Road, Momence, Ill., 60954
    (a periodical containing many additional sources of information)
Private Water Systems, Midwest Plan Service, Iowa State University, Ames,
    Iowa (a pamphlet, also available at local extension offices)

Recommended Books

Gene Logsdon, *Getting Food from Water: A Guide to Background Aquaculture*
    (Emmaus, Pa.: Rodale Press, 1978)
Tim Matson, *Earth Ponds: The Country Pond Maker's Guide to Building, Main-
    tenance, and Restoration* (Woodstock, Vt.: Countryman Press, 1991)
Tim Matson, *The Earth Ponds Sourcebook: The Pond Owner's Manual and
    Resource Guide* (Woodstock, Vt.: Countryman Press, 1991)
Henry David Thoreau, *Walden* (any edition)